RACE TO THE SKY

Discovering Your Soul Song and
Becoming the Person You Were Created to Be

Randy — many thanks for all you have done — looking forward to the journey ahead — Many blessings —

Rich Joy

RACE TO THE SKY

A True Story

RICH JOY

RACE TO THE SKY:
Discovering Your Soul Song and
Becoming the Person You Were Created to Be

Copyright © 2019 Rich Joy

No part of this book may be reproduced, stored in a retrieval system or transmitted in any form or by any means—electronic, mechanical, photocopy, recording or any other—except for brief quotations, without permission in writing from the author.

Cover design by Yvonne Parks at pearcreative.ca
Typesetting by Katherine Lloyd at theDESKonline.com

Printed in the United States of America

CONTENTS

Introduction		...1
Chapter One	THE LOST SONG	...3
Chapter Two	ALONE	...17
Chapter Three	NEW KID IN TOWN	...31
Chapter Four	WELCOME TO FEAR CITY	...47
Chapter Five	THE DARKNESS BEFORE DAWN	...5
Chapter Six	I THOUGHT I WAS ALIVE	...71
Chapter Seven	MY LAST GASP	...87
Chapter Eight	HITTING MY STRIDE?	...101
Chapter Nine	SURRENDERING TO MY SONG	...117
Chapter Ten	LEARNING HOW TO LOVE	...143
Acknowledgements		...161
About the Author		...163

INTRODUCTION

It's been said that you have to need a miracle in order to see a miracle. Well, I've seen many and needed more. Death threats, violence, danger, abuse, riots, gangs, mobsters, and more are all part of my story. So are divine intervention, prophetic encounters, mysterious spiritual moments, and supernatural healing.

But before I can tell you about the miracles, I need to dive into my desperate need for them. My life was once a long winter's darkness, trying to escape from one tragic event after another, longing for the hope of spring. My mother died when I was eleven, my father rejected me, and I found the streets of New York to be unwelcoming. This all led to decades of running in fear and burying my soul in a deep, dark cave where I couldn't hear its song.

Unable to hear the notes of my purpose, I chased hard after worldly achievement, interrupted by God in moments of need when I wasn't even looking for Him. He is truly the one who has rescued me. I had no role models to guide me other than the sitcom characters I saw on the sixteen-inch black-and-white box I watched as a child. Shows like *Leave It to Beaver* and *The Brady Bunch* gave me the only glimpses of how a family could or should be, and my life looked much more like the tragedies on the evening news.

I persisted in running, but God persisted more. He intervened to save my life again and again, and finally got through to me. God designed me for a purpose, and though I kept chasing pleasure, I ended up like Jonah. Running from his purpose didn't work for him, and it wasn't working for me. I finally realized that my purpose is to help others find theirs. I can finally hear my soul song and am working to help others hear theirs.

It's a choice I made but must continue to make—a choice to face my story. More than that, it's a choice to *share* my story, and in the process relive every detail, trusting God to meet me in each painful moment. I am astounded by how God has met me in these pages, and I trust He is going to meet you there too.

Chapter One

THE LOST SONG

Born in 1958, I arrived just in time to lose my sense of innocence at the same time America did. While I didn't choose to start my life in Queens, just outside New York City, I couldn't have picked a better place to guarantee life would not be easy.

To start, my father never wanted me. My birth was my mother's last-ditch effort to save an already bad marriage. On top of that, I was born the day my grandfather died. He was my dad's dad, and they never really knew each other. These might seem like small details, but they're the kind of details that often have much greater meaning in life.

Since my dad never really knew his father, he didn't talk much about him. The only story I know about him is that one day my Uncle Buddy (my dad's brother) went to work with their father on the George Washington Bridge. After that day, Uncle Buddy never went back. When my dad asked him why he quit the job, my uncle answered, "As we sat there taking a break, high up over the Hudson River, the men passed a bottle of whisky down the line of the steel beam we were sitting on. When they passed it to me, I took a sip to keep warm, like the rest of the men, and then turned to pass it on to the next man. But he was no longer there. He'd fallen into the Hudson."

My grandpa made a career of those jobs to provide for his family, and for years I didn't realize the inspiration he was to me as I faced my own difficulties. I was well into adulthood before I learned that I'd had a picture of him in my office for years—the famous picture of steel workers taking their lunch break hundreds of feet above New York City, while building the Rockefeller Center in 1932. This iconic photo captures the bravery and desperation of men who needed work during the Great Depression, and my grandpa is the one second from the left, lighting the cigarette of the man next to him.

That picture hung on my office wall, and I would tell people, "If I ever feel sorry for myself about working too hard, I look at this picture and remind myself how good I have it compared to these workers." Thousands of steel workers lost their lives during that time period in New York, just trying to put food on the table for their families.

To me, this picture represents the hopes and aspirations that millions of immigrants had in coming to this country. Their dreams were often dashed by the harshness of life. Their journey was one of tragedy and struggle, yet they faithfully went up on those steel beams to build one of the greatest cities in the world. They believed they could rise above their situation, and, in a symbolic way, they made a city rise up to be one of the greatest. New York was the gateway for millions of immigrants, all trying to exchange persecution, famine, and war, for freedom, democracy, and justice. It was a noble pursuit, and they worked nobly.

Grandpa Jim Joy second from left, lighting a fellow worker's cigarette

I had no idea, though, that one of the workers in that picture was my grandfather, Jim Joy, until twelve years ago when my older sister called me. "You know that picture of the guys on the steel beams, building that skyscraper?" she said.

"Sure. I've had it over my desk for over a decade," I replied.

"Those guys are role models of what America was built on—hard work."

"Well, the guy who's second from the left is our grandfather."

I couldn't believe it. I had used this picture to motivate me, to keep me thankful and working hard no matter what. It had inspired me to never give up. To confirm what she'd told me, I found an old photo of my grandfather from when he was about the same age as he was in that iconic photo. Sure enough, it was him—Jim Joy.

Things like this go beyond reasonable coincidence. As I said, I was born the day my grandfather died, and even though I never had a relationship with him, he inspired me throughout my life almost as if he was invisibly present. These are God's fingerprints, near-invisible markings of the divine. They are the reminders that my family curse of fatherlessness can be broken and replaced with a blessing.

And they are signs that each soul has a song that begins in past generations and carries on to future ones.

Every Soul Has a Song

Have you ever wondered if your soul has a purpose? I've seemingly always had a longing to know what I'm supposed to be doing during my limited time here on earth. While some people figure out what they want to do at an early age, others spend years and years stuck in life without ever finding that purpose. Many others' songs get buried due to trauma they experienced in life; that is what happened to me.

THE LOST SONG

One of my favorite depictions of discovering our purpose in life comes from a legend about an African tribe. Many versions of this legend have become popular, but I like this one:

> There is a tribe in Africa where the birth date of a child is counted not from when they've been born, nor from when they are conceived but from the day that the child was a thought in its mother's mind. And when a woman decides that she will have a child, she goes off and sits under a tree, by herself, and she listens until she can hear the song of the child that wants to come. And after she's heard the song of this child, she comes back to the man who will be the child's father, and teaches it to him. And then, when they make love to physically conceive the child, some of that time they sing the song of the child, as a way to invite it.
>
> And then, when the mother is pregnant, the mother teaches that child's song to the midwives and the old women of the village, so that when the child is born, the old women and the people around her sing the child's song to welcome it. And then, as the child grows up, the other villagers are taught the child's song. If the child falls, or hurts its knee, someone picks it up and sings its song to it. Or perhaps the child does something wonderful, or goes through the rites of puberty, then as a way of honoring this person, the people of the village sing his or her song.
>
> In the African tribe there is one other occasion upon

which the villagers sing to the child. If at any time during his or her life, the person commits a crime or aberrant social act, the individual is called to the center of the village and the people in the community form a circle around them. Then they sing their song to them.

The tribe recognizes that the correction for antisocial behavior is not punishment; it is love and the remembrance of identity. When you recognize your own song, you have no desire or need to do anything that would hurt another.

And it goes this way through their life. In marriage, the songs are sung, together. And finally, when this child is lying in bed, ready to die, all the villagers know his or her song, and they sing—for the last time—the song to that person.[1]

Whether or not this legend is true of an actual tribe, I believe it expresses truth. Each of us does have a song that is inseparable from our soul. It has taken me a long time, but I'm beginning to hear and live my soul's song. It was always there, in some ways even before I was born. God has been singing it over me and watching over my life to bring about moments when I would realize just how much my life was out of touch with the song it was meant to be.

But what else could I do? In a sense, my mom sang my song

---

[1] Alan Cohen, "A Child's Song," *Pathways to Family Wellness*, http://pathwaystofamilywellness.org/Letters-from-the-Editor/a-message-from-our-editor-issue-33.html.

for me early in life, but when she died, I had no one to remind me who I was born to be. I had no one to guide me and didn't know what else to do, so I ran from my song, just like I ran from God. I hid my song so deep inside that I couldn't remember what it was or where to find it.

The First Trauma

My idea of family wasn't shaped by my family; it was shaped by television shows like *Leave It to Beaver* and *The Andy Griffith Show*. As a child, I couldn't separate reality from fiction, so when I saw supportive, loving families portrayed on TV, I expected life to be the same. Sure, the families in these shows faced their own kinds of difficulties in every episode, but they always overcame them, and whenever there was conflict, they made it right and restored relationship before the episode was done. They still lived happily ever after, and more than that, they had a moral to the story to guide the viewer so he or she could also live happily ever after.

How disappointing it was, then, when my mom was diagnosed with cancer. I was only five and couldn't grasp the magnitude of that word. By the time I was seven, however, I had horrific memories, watching as doctors slowly removed part after part of my mother's body. The medical profession didn't yet understand the complexities of cancer, and each operation only prolonged the inevitable. Every time the cancer returned. I watched my mom lose body parts, hair, and weight until she weighed just seventy-nine pounds.

The numerous operations and hospital visits became a daily

ritual for me. Countless times I arrived at the hospital to learn that an operation had taken another part of my mom's body. As most people who've lost a loved one to cancer can tell you, watching my mother die such a slow death was haunting. Just as the doctors had no way to ease the disease, I had no way to ease my trauma.

Why did she have to suffer every day for so many years? My mom had taken me to the Catholic church for as long as I could remember, and I couldn't help but question God. Even then I held out hope and prayed for her to live. Oh, how I prayed for her to live!

Mom's Death

When people want to study writing about suffering, they look to Thomas Hardy novels, but anyone who wants to study suffering could do so just by looking at the day of my mom's funeral. I was living the last pages of the final chapter of my very first love.

The cold day contained no light for me, filled with emptiness, death, and despair. Clouds, steel gray and ominous, silhouetted the casket as the priest said the final words: "Let us commend Anneliese Joy to the mercy of God. We therefore commit her body to the ground; earth to earth, ashes to ashes, dust to dust; in the sure and certain hope of the resurrection to eternal life."

The words cut through the bitter March air of that New York day and remained frozen in time, etched on the pages of my mind: *Hope of the resurrection to eternal life.* What could that mean to an eleven-year-old whose mother had just died?

I wasn't aware that my breath had slowed. It was in harmony

with the season, which also seemed to be dead. As the ropes slid into the frozen earth, I felt my soul slip into the dark, cold grave along with the casket that contained my mother's lifeless body.

God isn't real, I told myself. For six years, every night in my prayers I had pleaded with God to save her life.

After my mom's death, I had no fight left with which to keep my own soul alive. All my fight had gone into trying to keep her alive, and I had nothing left for myself. I didn't see any point to it anyway. Doing so felt as hopeless as wishing my mother back to life while watching her being lowered into the grave.

That day couldn't have communicated my grief any more perfectly. The cold, the clouds. Even hail. It felt like an insult. Every stinging pellet of hail that hit my face reminded me that I was alive, despite how dead I felt inside.

As I stood shivering by the graveside, my mind tried to find order in my world—a world filled with the reminders of death. My body became numb to the cold, and my spirit became numb to the realities of life. At this young age, I was incapable of understanding what had happened and couldn't process the deep pain. Questions raced through my mind. Where would I go? What would I do? The unknown left me panicked and consumed with worry.

No Help Anywhere

No one came to answer my questions or to defend God. The bus ride my first day back to school was dreadful. While taking an empty seat in the back of the bus, I felt uneasy and different.

RACE TO THE SKY

All the kids avoided me. I sat there staring out the window with my mind drifting far away. I remembered just a few days before when my mom had been ushered out of our house on a gurney, dead. One day she was alive and then I lost her, the only person who cared about me.

I continued staring aimlessly out the window. It felt like an eternity as I sat there with no one speaking to me. I felt like a freak. The contrast couldn't have felt sharper—the other kids laughing and playing around on their way to school while I sat there empty and lonely inside. That's when I realized for the first time that I was now the kid whose mom had just died. That was now my label, whether I liked it or not.

Why me? Why did it have to be me? Had I been a bad kid? Was this my punishment, living like an outsider who can only peek into this world? It reminded me of when I attended Catholic school and my type of humor, acting as the class clown, was less than welcome. On many occasions I would be caught disrupting class, and that resulted in a nun chasing me around the classroom. When finally cornered, the nun would hit me with her fists. The blows that landed hurt, and deep inside I believed I deserved it. So did I do something to deserve my mom's death too?

Or maybe it wasn't my fault. Maybe it was the fact that my dad was lost in the bottle and couldn't even show up for himself, so maybe my mom was better off not being subjected to his alcoholic behavior? Regardless of why my mom died, the fact remained that I was truly alone, except for my dog, Bailey, my faithful companion. Even my older sister left home, escaping the fate that lay ahead for me.

THE LOST SONG

When I arrived at school, I still couldn't focus and just stared out the window in a daze. I could hear words being spoken, but it was as if I was in another place. I had no one to help me understand grief, no one to walk me through how to process my questions and emotions. Schools didn't have guidance counselors then, and no one talked about internal pain. My world had stopped when my mom died—leaving me with questions of why I was here and what would happen to me—but the world kept moving on without me.

Riding home on the bus that day, my mind continued drifting. I reflected on the night of my mom's funeral, how my cousins made fun of me, saying, "You don't have a mother! You don't have a mother! Why are you so sad? Are you a baby? You're a baby—a baby and now you're mad!" They sang it like a rhyme again and again, mocking me. My schoolmates treated me differently too. They didn't know how to act toward me, and I didn't understand why they were so mean. Instead of compassion or empathy, I received just the opposite, and I didn't know how to respond to them either.

I couldn't wait to get home to my bedroom. Coming home to an empty house proved even more lonely, but as I ran up the stairs and shut the door to my room, I felt safe and far away from the world. That's where I would find refuge in music.

Which album to choose today? Only one song fit the bill just right. It had to be the Beach Boys' forty-five, "In My Room." This song spoke exactly what my heart needed in my loneliness, singing about that one private place to hold your secrets, to protect you from worries and fears, where you can dream, pray, cry, and laugh freely. Each time the forty-five abruptly ended and made that screeching noise, I would move the needle back and play the song again.

On that cold, gray late-winter day, I was alone and unprepared to set out into the world by myself. Lying on my floor, I would think back to the times with my mom when I felt the most special, the most exhilarated, and the most alive. But memories could only do so much to soothe me. The reality was that I went from feeling like I was the center of the universe to realizing I was completely alone.

I'd been having intense nightmares from the time I was two years old, but now they changed. In one nightmare I was being smothered or choked, and in another I heard my mom groan in agony as she drowned from her fluid-filled lungs. The nightmares were bad enough, but the bigger problem was that, night after night, I was reliving what had actually happened. Each night, my mom's death replayed in my mind.

Where Is God?

When my mom died, I decided God wasn't real, but that didn't stop me from being angry with Him for allowing her to die. It would have been one thing if her death had been quick and painless, but she suffered for five years; it was torturous. I heard her cough relentlessly each night, hacking up the fluid that eventually killed her. My nightmares grated on me and were as real to me as her actual death.

During my mom's prolonged illness and amid the nightly

ritual of listening to her agony, I got little sleep. My memories haunted me. I was exhausted and felt responsible for not being able to help or somehow heal her. Maybe I hadn't prayed right. I wasn't sure, but based on what I'd read on my own and learned in Sunday school, God was supposed to heal her. Why didn't He? And if He was supposed to heal her but didn't, then He couldn't be real.

Why didn't God answer my prayers? That question remained with me every waking hour of every day. My mom was everything to me. Always there for me. My guiding light. My inspiration. And now she was gone.

Completely Alone

Just as present was my questions about how an eleven-year-old would take care of himself. Those questions, my fear of being alone, and the image of my mother's casket being lowered into the hail-swept ground plagued my mind and fueled my insomnia. My only escape was listening to music.

On some nights, instead of tossing and turning in bed, I listened to another Beach Boys forty-five—side A, "Wouldn't It Be Nice," and then side B, "God Only Knows." Side A's lyrics offered the hope that love existed, but the lyrics on side B reminded me that my mom had left me. It also reinforced the lingering question in my mind: If God was real, why did He let my mom die?

Oddly enough, although isolated and alone, I felt safe. The music carried my soul to a subterranean cave, away from the rest of the world. Finally feeling safe, and with the conflicting thoughts from sides A and B running through my mind, I would drift off to sleep.

The sound of the school bus often woke me in the morning and alerted me that I was late for school. On those days, I threw on my disheveled clothes and ran outside. Some days I made it to the bus stop, other days I wasn't so lucky. On the days when I arrived in time, I stared out the window at nothing. Everything was cold, dark, and gray; there was no hope on the horizon. My soul, my song, what God created me to be, was hidden from the world and might never see the light of day again.

Chapter Two

ALONE

You might reasonably ask, "Where was your dad? Why didn't he help you when your mom died?" They're legitimate questions. Many children have received comfort from a loving and caring father during their mother's illness and after her death, but my father had become a raging alcoholic to avoid his own pain.

When my mom was home from the hospital, I would hear her suffering and often told my dad she was writhing and crying. I waited for him to do something—anything—to help, but he only cursed at me while slumped in a recliner with an empty bottle of booze by his side. "Shut up and go to sleep!" he'd tell me. I had nowhere to turn, nowhere to go, and no one to help me or my mother. In bed, I listened to her cry out all through the night. Her pain became my pain as I felt my soul slowly slip away.

RACE TO THE SKY

After her death, I was left with an absentee, alcoholic dad who didn't seem to care that I needed to eat. With no food at home, I would scrape up three pennies from wherever I could find them to buy a small carton of milk at school. With no food to go with it, the milk would curdle in my stomach and I would run to the bathroom to vomit the curdled milk. The lonely jar of pickles in the refrigerator at home provided little sustenance.

Fear crept in and began to consume my mind. My dad was a New York City policeman. What if he were to get killed? I would be an orphan. Every day I faced neglect, periodic beatings, and verbal abuse to remind me I wasn't loved, and yet for a while I still had a tiny bit of hope. Deep down, I dreamed about my dad rising to the occasion and being a good single parent. But this fear of being alone was the last straw. It meant I no longer had any luxury of hope.

This was when I realized I had no one there for me, which meant one thing: I could only count on myself. One night when I was especially hungry, helpless, and alone, I pounded my fists on the floor of my bedroom, saying again and again, "I can only count on myself. I can only count on myself. There is no one to help me."

I was only eleven years old at the time. I couldn't carry the weight of being unwanted and unloved, let alone the weight of my grief, loss, and fear. My soul became my enemy because it made me feel. I couldn't fight hunger, loneliness, grief, and pain, so I had to fight my soul. I had to wall myself off—hide away on a remote island, hardened against anything that might hurt me.

ALONE

I adopted Simon and Garfunkel's "I Am a Rock" as my theme song to help guard me from pain. The Beach Boys sang of my room being a sanctuary, but that wasn't enough. I had to become a rock, an impenetrable fortress, with no need for friendship, laughter, or love.

Broken Expectations

I had good reasons to expect more from my dad. He was my dad, of course, but he was also a cop. Just as I knew what family should be like because of *Leave It to Beaver* and *The Andy Griffith Show*, I knew what police officers should be like because of *Dragnet*.

Growing up watching *Dragnet*, I was provided the idealistic, all-American version of a cop. The show's stories were real, but the names were changed to protect the innocent. In my story, no one was innocent, and my dad couldn't have been more unlike Officer Joe Friday.

My dad was a New York City cop in the 1960s and 1970s. At that time, being a cop in New York was a lot more like *Serpico* than *Dragnet*. If you don't know, the movie *Serpico* is about a New York City cop who refuses to take bribes, unlike the rest of the force. His partners place him in dangerous situations and his superiors ignore his accusations of corruption, so he goes public with the allegations. While the investigation takes place, he faces life with a target on his back as the cops try to kill him for being a snitch. It makes for an exciting story, but the thing is, it's based on a true story that happened while my dad was a cop.

I don't know whether my dad was on the take or not. Based on how poor we were, I'd like to believe he was clean, but the sad truth is I have no idea what kind of cop he was. I never had enough of a relationship with him to know. All I know is he fell far short of my hopes, expectations, and needs.

The Hero and the Mascot

As an adult, I've learned there's a name for what I did to cope. Children of alcoholics often take up one or more of four roles—the hero, the scapegoat, the mascot, or the good child. I became the hero and the mascot, which meant I tried to draw attention away from my dad by excelling in sports and cracking jokes.

As the hero, my hope was that I would be good enough to earn my dad's love and get him to stop drinking. As long as I could perform well enough, it helped me block the emotional pain from my trauma, disappointments, and unanswered prayers.

When I acted as the mascot, I received acceptance from my peers at school through humor, slapstick comedy, or getting in trouble. This acceptance helped take the focus off my problems and family dysfunction. I found that laughter was my connection to people and the world. From watching people like Bob Hope and Carol Burnette on TV, I learned that laughter was the solution for easing the pain in life, and at least this lesson learned from television didn't entirely disappoint me.

One thing that was completely lost in all this was my soul's song. At the time I didn't really know I had one, and I certainly never knew it was important to remember. Once my mom stopped fostering it in my life, all the noises of pain and need drowned out any care for who God created me to be or my deeper purpose in life. I had no idea what sense of fulfillment or belonging might be mine if I could just live that purpose. I had no idea I might even have a purpose. How could a child who knows he isn't wanted think he somehow had something as wonderful as a purpose?

These roles of being the hero and mascot followed me well into adulthood. My drive to excel in sports became a drive that led me to be a workaholic. My ability to make people laugh grew into an understanding of others' needs and a determination to meet them, even though I didn't understand my own. Through all of it, I was driven to show that my family was all right, no matter how far from the truth that was.

My sense of humor seemed like it was part of who I am, like it was in my DNA. While I had no connection to the father who gave it to me, my last name still is Joy. I've since done the research on my surname and discovered that some people with my family name were entertainers for the kings of England. Just like how my grandpa seemed to have been strangely with me, inspiring me for years without my knowing it was him, this ability for humor seemed to be bigger than me, somehow older and deeper than me, and yet an intricate part of who I was.

This performance, being the hero and the mascot, seemed to be working. My defenses were growing stronger and thicker, though often at the expense of others who bore the brunt of my inappropriate humor. I had no idea I was hindering others in their song. All I cared about was blocking out the pain, and I was becoming good at it.

Be the superhero. Save my family. Win in sports. Make people laugh. Don't let anyone see me cry. Just be a good kid. Do all of this, and my life would be good. Could it work?

I started to think so—until my stepmom came along.

Cinderella, Not The Brady Bunch

After my mom's death, my dad started seeing a lot of women; after all, it was the sexual revolution of the 1960s. One day he announced he was getting married. *Yes*, I thought, *There is hope.*

But once again, my hopes and expectations had been shaped by television, which really just shows how sorely I lacked real parents, teachers, or mentors to guide me. But I thought, *The Brady Bunch made it work. Maybe my dad will as well. Maybe my stepmom will be like the mom on the show.* The whole premise of *The Brady Bunch* was a blended family. A woman with three daughters meets a man with three sons, and they decide, according to the theme song, "that this group must somehow form a family."

Unlike Mike, the father on *The Brady Bunch*, my dad was an alcoholic. Also unlike the *The Brady Bunch*, he was marrying not homemaker Carol, but another alcoholic. And unlike on *The Brady Bunch*, my nightmare continued and became one of the stereotypical wicked-stepmother experiences.

Shortly into the marriage, my stepbrother was shipped off to a mental hospital and my older sister was thrown out of the house. Then it was announced that I could not be at home during the day because my stepmom wanted to run around the house naked. Paranoia was a side effect of her being an alcoholic and taking pills, and one day she also announced that I had masterminded a conspiracy against her. That, she said, was why she was losing her mind. Therefore, I was sent to the unfinished basement to sleep at night, and I could only come home at night and only eat what little food there was, but at least I had a place to sleep.

This was yet another hope that turned into great disappointment and despair for me. I desperately wanted to escape this environment. There had to be a better place, another way. Where could I go to find guidance? Where could I go for any help at all if no one was willing to step up? I didn't know where I would go, but the urge to run away plagued my mind every waking moment.

Where Are the Heroes?

If only someone had been there for me, I'm sure I would have run away as quickly as I could, but I didn't have anyone. No hero rose up to save me. I didn't even have a role model to simply be there for me. My only examples came from TV.

I found myself with no male mentors, no grandfather (my dad wouldn't allow my mom's father in my life), and a father who might as well have lived a thousand miles away. Being an alcoholic narcissist, he had no desire to be there for my sister or me. My mom's parents, whom my dad kept out of my life, were sure I would end up in jail. Considering the circumstances of my childhood, it's truly a miracle I never did end up there.

Kids generally think adults are fair toward children until they have an experience that proves otherwise. Being a good athlete, I was on the all-star baseball team. I could pitch, catch, or play outfield, but the coaches' sons were also on the all-star team, and I soon discovered that mattered more than skill did.

Though I could pitch, it was decided that another kid would pitch. This was a political decision, but I assumed it meant I would be catching; however, another boy was trying out for the catcher position. His dad was a coach too. This dad/coach, who was very tall, would stand directly behind the pitcher when it was my turn during the throw-out drill, blocking my view of second base. The goal of this drill was to throw out runners who were stealing second. Normally I would hit my target, but now my throws were wild since I couldn't see second base and was trying to throw over the head of the tall coach.

After field practice was batting practice, where everyone got twelve swings. I hit a homerun on my first swing and the same coach said, "That's enough. Sit down." I realized how unfair the world could be, not only in life but also in sports. No one was there for me, not even a fair coach on the all-star team. Instead of the coach uplifting and encouraging me through life, I felt undermined by adults I should've been able to trust.

How different things might have been if someone had just stepped up and been there for me, even during those handfuls of practices. Mentoring is simple yet profound in its reach. It involves a good man showing up consistently in a boy's life, assuring him another man cares for him and giving him a reference point of what it means to be a good man. Just knowing there is a man a boy can trust to show up will increase his self-worth and improve his relationships. He will likely do better at school and will be less inclined to get involved in crime and abuse.

Men often ask what difference one man can make. One man can't save the world, but he can make a world of difference in one boy's life. And when that boy becomes a man, he will know how to positively impact others in the same manner.

I never had a man stand up for me. Through experiences like these, people's hidden agendas became transparent. Other coaches in my life were verbally abusive and unsupportive. The lack of anyone willing to be a role model for me reinforced the belief that I could only count on myself.

Being alone and facing so much constant uncertainty, fear had been part of my life for a long time, but now it was different. It began to wrap itself around my mind like never before. It intensified and created a powerful drive within me to survive. My biggest problem, and the greatest fuel for my fears, was I didn't know whether I could survive, and I felt I had little choice in whether I would.

A Predator Attacks

My fear for survival was no hyperbole. One experience, above all in those years, proved just how narrow the difference might be between survival and death.

I was thirteen, and a sexual predator lurked near my school.

He had already attacked both students and teachers, and no one had been able to stop him yet.

One day, he attacked me. He seemed to come out of nowhere. He was over six feet tall and I was no match. In his choke hold, I could barely breathe as he held me with one hand and put a knife to my throat with the other. "If you move, I'll slit your throat," he hissed at me.

Shock and fear engulfed me. Unable to breathe, I couldn't scream. And even if I had been able to scream, there probably wouldn't have been anyone around to help me.

As the man tried to have his way with me, a moment came when I had a chance to escape, and I took it. That single quick decision might have saved my life.

The predator chased after me, but I ran until I came across a woman and her daughter. I kept myself away from the predator by using them as a screen. He realized there were now witnesses and disappeared.

I went to the police to report what happened, but since the predator hadn't been able to actually finish his intended rape, the detective who interviewed me was confused about whether there was a crime to be prosecuted. "If nothing happened, then we cannot prosecute," he told me.

I looked down and shook my head. "No, nothing happened."

"Well, then there's nothing we can do. Did you know that teachers in your school and children in the neighborhood have been raped by him? So are you sure nothing happened?"

The detective asked the question again. I hesitated, thinking over the attack. While the full act didn't happen, there was the attempt. I answered, "Well, I guess something really did happen. I mean, well …" and I went into detail.

"Okay, let's take down this statement," the detective said. "Your name?"

"Richie."

"How old are you?"

"I am thirteen years old."

"What did the suspect look like? Can you describe him to us?"

I did the best I could.

They kept asking more questions to fill out their report. What time did this happen? Where did it happen? What did he say to you? Did he attack you? Did he have a weapon?

While the detective took the report, other officers had taken a squad car to the area I described. The perpetrator was hanging around there searching for another victim, and they picked him up and brought him in for a lineup.

After I answered each question in detail, they brought me to another area and asked if I could pick out the perpetrator in a lineup. I agreed, and as I peered through the window at a lineup of men who all looked like the suspect, I pointed and blurted out, "That's him!"

"Are you sure?" the detective asked.

I nodded. "Yes. That's definitely him."

A Hero Is Born

Over a year went by, and each day I was picked up from school by a detective who then escorted me home. This seemingly endless situation was leading up to me taking the stand in the predator's trial. My nerves were racked, and the fear and humiliation of taking the stand wore on me.

I had told my father what had happened, but he never brought it up again. Not even a knife to my throat and almost being raped could stir him to act like a real father. He was nowhere to be found and I was on my own. I had no one to talk to except the detectives, but they were interested only in the facts and prosecuting the perpetrator. The toll of keeping everything inside wore on me day after day.

Finally, the agonizing day came. I went in front of the grand jury to once again talk about what had happened. I sat there, slumped over, testifying for the grand jury, devastated by the overwhelming sense of emptiness that came from being so completely on my own through it all. Being alone while facing another trauma on top of all the trauma I'd already experienced felt like hell on earth.

On the stand, at times my voice sounded young and terrified as I relived how I had been jumped and dragged into an alley behind the school, had a knife at my throat, and was almost raped. At other times, my voice rang out brave and resilient. I was a boy protecting other teachers and vulnerable children. It was time to get justice for the ones who couldn't endure the stress of the trial. I had to be strong for all of them. The hero child had to save the people, and this criminal had to be put away. After all, that was what heroes did on TV.

I did what I could, and the fate of the matter was now in the hands of the grand jury. Would my case go to trial or be dismissed? The time that passed while we waited for the results is a blur, but the grand jury determined there should be a trial.

The courts were backed up, so this meant even more waiting. When the trial finally came, another year later, I sat outside the jury room, waiting day after day to take the stand. I had to keep coming back to the courthouse because I never knew when I would be needed. Every trip to the trial I made alone, and then I had to sit there, waiting, alone.

The trauma of being alone—along with the fear of facing the rapist again, and facing his friends, the jurors, and the attorneys by myself—had my nerves raw. I thought about my statements against this man who I wanted put away in federal prison for life. It was my job to go through with this, be the hero, and get the predator off the street. After all, who else would do it? I might have been a kid, but I thought I could be a superhero just like the ones I grew up watching on TV. These thoughts became my only comfort and strength amid constant fears.

Minutes felt like hours, as I dreaded the moment they would call me in. Even with the fear of the unknown courtroom, it was too late to turn back now. Why had I gone to the police station? I felt helpless, and my hands sweated and trembled. I fumbled with the papers in my hands. My heart was pounding. My breathing was short. Muddled thoughts filled my mind as my vision blurred.

The door to the jury room finally opened. A man came out and said it was over.

"What do you mean it's over?" I asked in disbelief. "Is the predator free to go?"

"No. Your attorney will come and explain it to you. You don't have to go in and testify."

I sat there in shock, relieved but confused. Minutes went by, which again seemed like hours. Many thoughts raced through my mind. *Will he be out in a year? Maybe two? Will he stalk me and kill me for this?* Fear kept me on edge until the district attorney finally came in.

"It's over, Richie," he told me. "We sent him away. You did such a good job testifying to the grand jury that the rapist's public defender took the deal they offered him."

"Deal? What deal?" I stuttered.

"The public defender convinced him to take a plea bargain down to a twenty-year deal in a federal prison."

I had wanted a life sentence, but still felt like I'd won and that twenty years was as good as life. Slumped over, relieved, still sweating, I was now exhausted but victorious in putting him away. I'd done it. I'd sent a predator away to a federal penitentiary, even if it cost me more of my innocence.

I had done it alone, but I had done it. In my mind, I'd done something right for humanity. I became the hero, not a victim. Maybe, just maybe, that meant I could survive being alone in New York after all.

Chapter Three

NEW KID IN TOWN

One mark of growing up in an unhealthy environment is the constant need to adapt. Healthy parents create stability for their family, so their children don't question, "Will I have a home to live in?" "Will I get enough food today?" or "Does anyone care about me?" After my mom died, I had no one to answer these questions for me. I could only rely on myself.

The constant instability around me was, of course, unpredictable. I never knew what unexpected need would come up and change how I would have to take care of myself. Again and again, just when I thought I was getting on top of my needs or my circumstances, they would change and I would be under them all over again.

This instability is a trauma by itself—the ever-present need to adapt, never knowing whether what worked today would still work tomorrow, never trust anything or anyone.

Having gained a sense of heroism from walking alone through the difficult trial, putting a rapist in prison, and protecting who knows how many teachers and children, I felt like I was starting to get on top of life again. But I couldn't control everything else, and I soon needed to adapt all over again, beginning with losing my one remaining bright spot in life.

Despite all the difficulties I'd been through, I had always been able to count on my childhood best friend—my dog, Bailey. He'd been there for me every day from the time I was five years old, always happy to see me. He was playful, a loyal companion who could completely change the way I felt, and he could calm me when the anxiety of my circumstances became overwhelming.

Soon after my dad remarried, we moved to a new house. This house was closer to New York City and had a very small backyard. Bailey had always come to life when I came home from school, but now he would greet me with a broken, disheartened spirit. I believe he could feel the despair of the new situation we were in.

One day, I came home from school and Bailey was gone. When I asked about him, I was told that my dad had taken him to the pound to have him put to sleep. They told me it was better for him that way, but I knew it really was just one more thing to get rid of to make my dad and his new wife's lives easier.

I figured the next things on their list to get rid of were my sister and me. Sure enough, my sister soon left home because my dad and his new wife wanted to charge her a large sum of money to rent a room in their house. That strategy worked well for them since it was basically the equivalent of kicking her out of the house. Years later, I learned that I didn't have to worry about this, though it was for a terrible reason. My aunt told me that my sister and I had family who had cared about us this whole time and wanted to adopt us, but my dad wouldn't allow it.

It wasn't because he loved us, but because he wanted to continue receiving the Social Security checks from my mom's death. Losing us would mean losing his drug and alcohol money. Keeping us around was what let him take his wife to lavish dinners while leaving me with little to no food to eat.

New Way to Be Cool

Losing Bailey meant I was truly alone. There was no one—no pet, no person, nothing—here in this life for me. My dad even took all the money in my piggy bank—my source of three-cent milk money—declaring he needed it for some reason.

Psychologists have identified thirteen primary categories of childhood trauma, and by age thirteen I had experienced eleven of them. My latest setback of losing Bailey made me even more desperate to fit in with the cool group at my new school. I'd lost my friend at home, so I needed friends somewhere else. In my previous neighborhood and school, excelling in sports was enough to fit in, but in this new school I needed to do more. I began smoking pot and drinking alcohol, which also served to medicate the pain I endured.

As this internal pain increased, a new identity grew in my heart. I now felt like an orphan, abandoned on a whole new level. I had no connection to the boy my mother had loved. That boy, his song, and his soul were all buried under so much pain I couldn't find him anymore. Instead of searching for who God made me to be, I divorced myself from my true self, even to the point of taking a new name.

My mother had called me Rick, but Rick was gone, so at my new school I introduced myself as Richie. Rick was a kid's name, fit for discarding along with the naïve idealism I had about life from my old favorite TV shows. Richie was older and cooler, more deserving of acceptance from the only group that might tell me I somehow belonged. Little did he know what harsh realities of life lay ahead for him.

Belonging was really the point. A person can only bear being alone for so long. I could play sports and was a good athlete because I enjoyed it, but I needed someone to accept me. I sacrificed myself to find a sense of family, just as some kids do in joining gangs.

Finding Anything Like Life

For most youth who experience trauma, puberty will either be delayed or accelerated. In my case, it was accelerated. For teenagers who already feel stigmatized by trauma, the loss of control over their bodies with the onset of puberty may add the difficulty of feeling physically awkward around their peers.

As well, adolescents who are particularly sensitive to stress because of trauma are more vulnerable to feeling overcome by fear or aggression. That aggression might be directed at others, such as through fighting or online bullying, or toward themselves, such as abusing substances, engaging in self-harm, or putting themselves in dangerous situations. For young adults, earlier or repeated trauma may impair the development of social and sexual relationships.[1]

Since I didn't know how to process all the stress and trauma, sexual relationships with girls in high school became a passion, in addition to using pot and alcohol. Since I loved everything about women and they liked me, I filled my void for love with sex. At the time, getting any kind of female affection seemed to fill my need to replace my mom.

Another common side effect of trauma I experienced was trouble thinking clearly, reasoning, and problem solving. I had difficulty adjusting to change because it required me to take in new information and consider multiple perspectives. It was hard for me to maintain attention and curiosity, especially when I was distracted by traumatic images or associations. When I received multiple instructions simultaneously, I became overwhelmed and had trouble concentrating. All of these issues are common in children who've experienced trauma, but, again, I didn't know any of this then. I only knew the difficulties I had to work through—or, as more often happened, run from.

---

[1] Please see https://childhoodtraumarecovery.com/ for articles by psychologist and childhood trauma survivor David Hosier MSc on effects of childhood trauma on mental health, therapies, self-help and related topics.

Running was all I knew how to do. It was either that or sink into a world of darkness and negativity, and I didn't see that as an option. I had to stay positive—overly positive—to keep going after anything that felt like life. But constant running kept me from truly knowing myself. I couldn't self-evaluate accurately, which not only hurt me in school but also—and more importantly—kept me from seeing the ways God kept trying to sing my soul's song over me.

I couldn't hear my song; I could only hear the song of fear.

A New Kind of Fear

Part of growing up in the Civil Rights era meant kids from the ghetto were bused in to my new school. The government leaders who ordered this had good intentions. They wanted racial integration, which is maybe what happened in the long term, but in the short term, it created a tremendous amount of racial tension. After all, it was the 1970s in the American Northeast and racial tension was at an all-time high in our country.

I became friends with a black girl, and asked her one day, "Why are there always fights and problems between blacks and whites?"

"Blacks don't hate you as a person. They just hate you because you're white," she said. "You have to understand that our grandparents were slaves." This made sense to me, but it didn't change the reality of being in a racially charged war zone.

Race riots were prevalent in the 1970s. Between 1964 and 1977, at least twenty-two major race riots took place in and

NEW KID IN TOWN

around New York City.[2] The atmosphere was continuously charged, and busing black kids in to a mostly white high school made the situation even more volatile.

This made my survival more complex. Now life was not just about food and belonging, but also about real survival—racial tension, prejudice by both whites and blacks, and not getting mugged, knifed, or killed. These were all very real possibilities where I lived. Muggers don't care who you are; they just want your money, and maybe your life as well. Gangs don't care who you are either; they only care whether you're in the wrong place at the wrong time, and they get to tell you when and where that is. Even a race riot doesn't care who you are or whether or not you're prejudiced or racist. It doesn't care if you're friends with black people. In true irony, a race riot often only cares about what color your skin is, and mine is white. For all these reasons, staying alive became the new theme of my life.

Run for It

The summer of 1974 came, and I was sixteen. The need to earn money to survive led me to get a job in the city. New York City was in great turmoil. Crime rates soared. I hoped getting a job would give me a new life and freedom from hell, but instead I had to learn to survive in one of the hardest places to live in the

---

[2] "Mass racial violence in the United States," *Wikipedia*, https://en.wikipedia.org/wiki/Mass_racial_violence_in_the_United_States#Civil_rights_movement:_1955%E2%80%931973.

world. It was a jungle and I had no real skills. What I did know was how to run fast, show up, and work hard.

My job was working as a gopher in a construction company, which meant they would say, "Hey, kid, go 'pher' this," and, "Hey, kid, go 'pher' that." I would ride the Long Island Rail Road and then catch the subways, being sent all over New York City. Each job I was sent on exposed me to the underbelly of the city. Each step made me feel more afraid of the dark side of life.

The areas I was sent for work in and around the city were crime-filled hell holes known as Harlem, Bedford–Stuyvesant, and Hell's Kitchen—some of the worst places in New York during the 1970s. The Big Apple was now a rotten apple. Once known as the financial capital of the world, it was now bankrupt. The neighborhoods I frequented were filled with riots, muggings, and countless homicides.

It certainly wasn't an experience for any child. My bosses would tell me that I did the work of two people. When I would return at noon, already completing the full day's work, they would tell me they didn't know what to do with me next.

What they didn't know was that I was living in fear. When I left the front door of their office in Long Island City, just across from the 59th Street Bridge, I would run full speed to the subway. Long Island City was no exception to all the violent crime in those days. I would run in fear every workday, and then keep running for most of my life.

My bosses would send me on a subway to this neighborhood

and that neighborhood, where I would then find out they were the worst ghettos in New York City and the surrounding areas. I had no option but to run through these neighborhoods as fast as I could to finish whatever job I'd been given. The reality was, though, no matter how fast I ran, there was nowhere to hide from the inevitable insanity of a city in complete and utter chaos.

Boom boxes blaring around the city gave off a variety of vibrations, mostly conveying negative messages that this was a world of survival of the fittest. Darwinian theory was alive and well in The Big Apple as dark ambiences of death and evil hovered over the streets like the sweltering heat rising from the beaten-down concrete jungle. The stench of garbage, urine, and filth filled the air. People were often mugged at knifepoint, including me on more than one occasion.

Living in constant danger forces people to develop survival skills. One skill I learned was to keep whatever money I had on me in my shoes. That way, I didn't lose everything if I did happen to get mugged. My other defense mechanism was to dress like a mugger. I would wear a t-shirt with ripped up jeans and work boots, and roll a pack of Marlboro cigarettes in my shirt sleeve. With a lit cigarette in my mouth, I would walk around looking as mean and tough as I could muster. Inside, though, I was a nervous wreck, afraid of everything around me.

The main survival skill I learned was to run, and I didn't just run from muggers and gangs. I ran from my own soul, from the song I was meant to live but had long forgotten.

RACE TO THE SKY

"I Have to Get Out"

There wasn't really any safe place in New York City during the 1970s. My job required me to take my life into my hands, but I cleared two hundred and fifty dollars per week, and in 1975 that was a lot of money for a sixteen-year-old. That money gave me hope of escaping my life and creating a new one.

My first step toward freedom came in the form of buying a car. As soon as I bought it, some kids in a Brooklyn ghetto flooded it. On a hot, muggy, one-hundred-degree day, the kids popped open a fire hydrant and funneled the water between the seams of my car's window, which was missing the rubber stripping between the back and front passenger-side windows.

Approaching my car, I feared it wouldn't start and I would be stuck in an area where crime was the worst in New York City. When I opened the door, water rushed out. I got in and gently turned the key. Thankfully the car started, although sluggishly, and I drove off with water sloshing around on the floorboards. This was when I concluded I had to escape from New York City at any cost. I didn't know how or where I would land; all I knew was I had to get out.

What Happened to New York?

My car was a gas guzzler, so somedays I would ride the train and subways to work, but I could only take so much of the subways. The graffiti everywhere comprised of words and images reflecting what hell must be like. The main themes were colorful curse

NEW KID IN TOWN

words and apathetic epithets. It cried out in a strangely uniform voice that life was hopeless, the city was a lost cause, and it was better to give the one-fingered salute to everything and everyone than to care about anything in this God-forsaken place. The nightly news confirmed new murders each day, so why wouldn't I be the next one to die in this hell hole?

How did one of the best cities in the world become so bad? New York City was reeling from a decade of social turmoil. In the 1970s, it fell into a deep tailspin provoked by the flight of the middle class to the suburbs. In addition, a nationwide economic recession hit New York's industrial sector, inhabitants, and civil servants especially hard.

This—combined with substantial cuts in law enforcement and firefighters, and citywide unemployment topping 10 percent—created civil unrest. Crime and financial crisis became the dominant themes of the decade, and I believed that life was like this everywhere. After all, with no other perspective on life, what other point of reference would one have at the age of sixteen? In just five years, from 1969 to 1974, the city lost over five hundred thousand manufacturing jobs, which resulted in over one million households being dependent on welfare by 1975. In almost the same span, rapes and burglaries tripled, car thefts and felony assaults doubled, and murders went from 681 to 1,690 a year.[3]

---

3 Kevin Baker, "'Welcome to Fear City' – the inside story of New York's civil war, 40 years on," *The Guardian*, May 18, 2015, https://www.theguardian.com/cities/2015/may/18/welcome-to-fear-city-the-inside-story-of-new-yorks-civil-war-40-years-on.

Depopulation and arson also had pronounced effects on the city. Abandoned blocks dotted the landscape, creating vast areas absent of urban cohesion and life itself. This was the world into which I was thrust, and my experience was one of sheer terror and trauma.

The graffiti-filled landscape I remember from New York.

It was a crime-filled, scary place to be, especially at night. I felt the heaviness and despair of this unsafe environment. As the summer went by, I became more and more zombie-like. Each day I lived in a state of shock, fear, and paranoia. In addition to the external trauma, I still had daily nightmares from the earlier years of my childhood. Fear became my identity by default, as I knew no other reality or way of being. No one was there to tell me that life could be different. Anything better than the crime-filled hell I'd always seen had to be just television fantasy.

Never-ending questions consumed my mind: *What will happen to me? Who will take care of me? Will I end up like the people on the streets and in the subways?*

The Hopeless Homeless

As I walked the streets (or, most of the time, ran through them) and rode the subways, I saw homeless people who lived below third-world-country standards. Some had soiled themselves as they slept on the seats of the subway day after day. The stench and horrendous sight kept anyone from trying to help them. The subway conductors displayed the only small measure of humanity I saw on the streets, by letting the homeless ride the subways all night long.

Petrified commuters were threatened by wheelchaired panhandlers who would give the look of death if money wasn't placed in their hat. It seemed clear these panhandlers were not crippled; I could see two healthy legs beneath the blankets over their laps. The man pushing the wheelchair looked like he just got out of prison. Some people would put money in the hat, fearing for their life, but most just ignored the homeless who clearly needed help.

It was a world turned upside down. The thought that I might wind up like these homeless people confirmed for me that life was truly about survival. I watched the same scene play out every day on the subways. Criminals could bully their way into an income, but homeless people had no hope. No true charity existed anywhere that I could see.

On the streets I ran to stay alive, and in life I ran to not end up like the people I saw on the streets. Images of drunken men in trench coats—passed out, drunk, with bottles of Thunderbird bum wine lying on their chest—reminded me that if I failed, a similar fate awaited me. Maybe I would be lucky and wind up like the bag ladies living from a shopping cart, sleeping on the streets. These realities of the city fueled a drive to work as hard as I could for the rest of my life. If I didn't, I could suffer their fate.

A Spiritual War Zone

New York was not just a physical and racial war zone. It was a spiritual war zone as well. If you go to Times Square today, you'll find blaringly bright advertisements and screens everywhere competing for your attention, a brilliant exclamation point of everything New York hopes to be. But if you went to Times Square in the 1970s, you would find wall-to-wall peep shows, prostitutes, and adult film stores.

This was a war where only the strong in the physical and the spiritual survived. When I was sent near Times Square, I had no point of reference on how to handle hookers who would approach me. One day one of the hookers was singing to me, "Come on, baby, I'm your momma, I'm your daddy, I'm your hooker in the alley. You want some sugar, honey?"

Not only did I have no point of reference for this, but I also had no money for it, even if I wanted to go with them. Many of the hookers were local women who had no other option to survive an unforgiving city. Others represented a cross-section of broken lives across America who happened to find their way to New York in hopes of making it big in the city.

The never-ending presence of prostitutes roaming the streets in various locations around the city continued to confuse me. I was conflicted; though I had the raging hormones of a teenager and wanted to have sex with them, I knew it was morally wrong. I never did engage them, instead feeling sorry for their plight. I would sing the Bruce Springsteen song "New York City Serenade" to myself—a song about walking tall and proud down Broadway with a prostitute on your arm.

The reality is that this was just another demonstration of how desperately people were struggling to survive and stay off the streets. It was another form of decaying human life, adding to the intense dissonance of watching it become normal for people to live in stench, garbage, and filth.

I was raised Catholic, and guilt was part of the package. Running into the peep shows that were lined up in Times Square just aggravated the confusion of whether God existed in this surreal world. If He didn't exist, then I had no reason to feel guilty, so why did I feel guilty?

I still had that old argument raging inside me—God can't be real, because God let my mom die. He allowed my dad to be a drunk. He let me be home alone with no food. I was too angry with God to care if He was real. I rebelled against God, life, and everything I thought my soul represented. On the other hand, I knew in the depths of my soul that sin in any form was wrong, no matter how it was justified.

So where had my soul gone? With all the conflict and trauma around me, my soul was successfully hidden away in the depths of a subterranean cave. The world was not a safe place to wear your soul on your sleeve.

Chapter Four

WELCOME TO FEAR CITY

It was around noon one summer day in 1975, a day I would never forget. Having finished my work at the construction company, I walked around Times Square looking for a place to eat. A pamphlet lay on the ground with a frightening cover that read "Welcome to Fear City: A Survival Guide for Visitors to the City of New York."

Now they tell me, I thought as I skimmed through it. It seemed like a joke, as one of the first few paragraphs advised, "Until things change, stay away from New York City if you possibly can." I shoved it into my back pocket and kept on walking.

Turning a corner, I walked into what looked like a set from a horror show. A gang had taken over one half of the street and was burning trash in a garbage can. I quickly walked to the other side of the street and ducked into a deli run by an Asian family.

RACE TO THE SKY

They watched me closely to determine if I was a gang member or a customer. After buying a Dr. Pepper, I bolted out the door and ran in the opposite direction back toward Times Square, away from the unruly gang that was obviously looking for trouble.

I turned down 6th Street and kept walking, observing all the crazy people and sights that adorned the circus that was real life in the city. After what seemed like at least a couple miles, I walked into Ray's Pizza, ordered a slice, and found a place to sit. Paper crinkled in my back pocket as I sat down, and I pulled out the pamphlet to read it while I waited.

Still believing it was a joke, I read a list of nine guidelines to get out of the city alive and without suffering loss. Visitors were advised to not take the subways or walk outside anywhere after six in the evening. Really, it advised tourists to not walk anywhere, especially alone, but to call taxis ahead of time instead.

The pamphlet went on to describe the extreme care visitors should take with their handbags, items left in vehicles, and possessions in general. Even hotel vaults were not to be trusted. With regard to hotels, the pamphlet warned that the fire department couldn't guarantee the safety of anyone, so visitors should "avoid buildings that are not completely fireproof" and "obtain a room that is close by the fire stairs." Later in life I found out these pamphlets were handed out by off-duty police officers at New York City airports in 1975.

The pamphlet read like the apocalypse described in the biblical book of Revelation. One article describing this era in New York said, "It's difficult to convey just how precarious, and paranoid, life in New York felt around that time. Signs everywhere warned you to mind your valuables, and to keep neck chains or other jewelry tucked away while on the subway."[1] This was absolutely true. I became hypervigilant, trying to notice where everyone on the street was. I made sure I walked near the gutter, giving me a good eight feet from any doorway or alley, and constantly looked over my shoulder to ensure I wasn't jumped from behind by someone lurking in the shadows. This became my way of trying to survive at work.

Then when I got to my place, I couldn't eat since the environment seemed entirely unnatural to how humans were supposed to live and be. I developed an ulcer from the stress.

The Filth and Stench of the City

The city hadn't been in good (or even decent) shape for years, but a deep financial crisis brought it to a new low. Simply put, New York City had racked up debt it couldn't pay. It was a freight train without brakes heading fast for the end of the tracks. Everyone knew it was happening, but even the federal government refused to help. Everyone outside the city had given up on it, and everyone inside the city lived accordingly.

The mayor's best solution to the budget crisis was to lay off tens of thousands of police and firefighters, creating a situation where either huge sections of the city couldn't be patrolled at all or the entire city was left insufficiently patrolled. So if a building caught on fire, it might burn to the ground before the fire

---

1 Ibid.

department could respond. Not only were many of our civil servants corrupt, having been bought by the mobs, but now there were even fewer people to do whatever good they did mean to do.

As a result, nearly every public space became a potential haven for crime. Gangs became bolder, stronger, and scarier. Burned-out and abandoned buildings made parts of town look like a war zone. Pornography flourished even in what were considered reputable neighborhoods, and drugs flooded the streets even more than before. A two-day garbage collector's strike left thousands of tons of garbage uncollected throughout the city. The entire city's existence felt unbelievable, like a dystopian novel, yet that's what I lived every day.

Celebrating the Bicentennial

It's difficult to give adequate perspective of just how much my environment affected me. I didn't have a solid base of family, friends, or community to keep me grounded to any particular reality. Most people have at least one of those three, even if their family breaks down, but I had nothing. Maybe if I'd been born in a nice, steady town, that could have given me some sort of grounding, I would've had that, but being in New York City placed me in the center of a culture swirling with massive and rapid transformation.

I felt the continued tearing away of our culture from its Victorian moral tradition. Our entire national culture and identity questioned everything at the time in my life when a more

WELCOME TO FEAR CITY

certain culture might have offered me the stability I needed, yet even there I was alone.

As well, by July 1975, even though the Vietnam War was officially over, the nation was far from unified in how it felt about this. Everyone seemed relieved, but while some celebrated the end of what they saw as evil or injustice, others grieved America's first war that failed to gain its objective. The tensions surrounding it were palpable, just as they had been throughout most of my years growing up.

As the calendar rounded the corner to 1976, and with the war over, there was hope that America might be able to take a break from all the turmoil to celebrate its historic Bicentennial Day on July 4. Early that morning I stumbled out of bed, and everything was eerily quiet as the sun rose.

One of the festivities planned was a procession of sailing ships—referred to as the Tall Ships—on the Hudson River. The plan was that the Statue of Liberty would welcome many ships parading on the river. That iconic statue had welcomed my mother's parents when they came over from Europe in the early 1920s, so for me, she conjured up great pride of being an American.

The day became a sweltering, muggy day. New Yorkers tried to forget their troubles and the troubles of the city. I tried to forget my troubles as well.

Some friends had invited me to go to the harbor with them, but despite the idea of the grandeur of this great celebration, the reality of taking the Long Island Rail Road and then the subway into Lower Manhattan so I could see the ships seemed like work. Sure, standing along the shoreline while eating a slice of pie from Ray's Pizza sounded enticing, but it wasn't enticing enough to get me to leave the comforting sound of the fan echoing off my bedroom walls.

July 4 celebration featuring New York's Statue of Liberty.

Instead, I watched it on television. It was an amazing event as the ships came, one by one, for what seemed like a couple of hours. Some of the ships were escorted upriver by an unofficial flotilla of pleasure craft of all sizes and shapes. A great festive atmosphere abounded, with crowds of people cheering.

Not everything about the day was as perfect as it seemed. The gritty underbelly of New York City reared its ugly head when a housewife was fished out of the harbor wearing bricks of heroin. It was a clear sign that gangs and Mafia were using the preoccupation of police that day to sneak in tens of millions of dollars of drugs, ready to hit the streets. Still, could the celebrations of this day really mean hope for New York? Could this be the day that I came back from the dead, just like the city?

Just the fact that a day like this could happen in New York City without major disaster meant it was a success. This was the largest gathering of sailing ships in New York Harbor since the 1800s, and ships were coming from all over the world.

What about the waterfront? I thought. *The piers are rotting for blocks, and no ship's been to those warehouses since World War II.* That whole part of town was cut off from the rest of Manhattan by the rusting hulk of the closed West Side Highway.

But then came the ships. They were magnificent as they passed by the Statue of Liberty. As I watched on TV, I thought about my grandparents who had come to Ellis Island in 1922. I considered how they must have felt leaving Europe and seeing this great statue that offered them a new opportunity and hope of a better way of life. Since it stood for Liberty Enlightening the World, I felt my world could be enlightened if I could just figure out how to make that change—how to escape New York. How ironic that what once represented hope for all those entering New York now reminded me how my only hope was in leaving the city.

As I watched the remaining large boats sail past the Statue of Liberty and up the Hudson, the TV showed everyone cheering and fireworks going off all around her. This incredible sight gave me hope that my life could be revived, that I could escape.

RACE TO THE SKY

It gave me hope that I, too, could be free from the chains of fear that I would not survive the Rotten Big Apple that summer.

My plan was to escape by the end of that summer, with the hope that college would offer a new way of life. I had calculated that by the end of August, I would have enough money to make it into this new life.

Chapter Five

THE DARKNESS BEFORE DAWN

Seeing college as my ticket out of New York wasn't any sort of brilliant inspiration; it was just simply the most obvious option. My construction job made me fear for my life, so I didn't want a career from that. I didn't see any other legitimate options anywhere around town either. That had been a key part of my problem for years—I didn't see options for any kind of life in New York City, at least not any kind of life I wanted.

In my biggest attempt to run from my problems yet, I enrolled in college. Somehow, I even graduated from high school at the age of seventeen to make it happen as soon as I could. My construction job that summer had enabled me to save up enough money for one year of college. But just like anything else in my life up to that point, I couldn't manage to find the easy way.

With little money and only a duffle bag containing all I owned, I hitched a ride to Upstate New York from Long Island, discovering upon arrival to campus that I was the last one to get to my dorm room. I never got the letter telling me to be there a week earlier for freshman orientation. Now I worried, having no clue of what college was going to be like.

Since I was the last one to arrive, I got the top bunk in a three-person dorm room that was a sprawling fourteen-by-fourteen space. Sharing space for clothes, I got the bottom drawer of a dresser. My roommates stared as I dumped the contents of my duffle bag onto the floor, then stuffed everything into the drawer before shoving the drawer back into the dresser. *Perfect*, I thought, having unpacked my belongings in less than a minute.

I thought I was all set to begin college. What I didn't know, despite all my years in school before then, was that I had dyslexia; I had just thought I was stupid. This didn't bode well for the program I registered for—premed dental, filled with math and science classes. By November I was failing out. I pretty much stopped going to class. The local bars were more fun, and sleeping in with a hangover was easier than going to classes I didn't understand.

I should have never been in a premed schedule of classes. Being so naïve, when I went to sign up for classes, they asked me what I wanted to be, and I simply said a dentist. That idea made sense, since I needed dental work and I thought a dentist would make a lot of money. The reality, however, was I would fail all my math and science classes that first semester, with the highlight being a D in zoology.

The Darkness of Winter

As the weather in Upstate New York turned dreary and cold, I became more depressed. Right before Thanksgiving of 1976, the temperature became unseasonably cold, and along with that came thoughts of committing suicide.

By that point, failing out of my first semester was inevitable. The cafeteria food was so bad that I just drank milk. The weather was unusually harsh leading up to the blizzard, and I lost weight from not eating and not wanting to leave my dorm room.

The average temperature for November and December that year was about eleven degrees below normal. That trend continued in January, with temperatures ten degrees below normal. This made conditions miserable, especially when the thirty-mile-per-hour (or more) winds sent the wind chill plummeting further.[1]

This wasn't just a colder-than-normal winter in Upstate New York; it also saw record-breaking snowfall. By November we had received thirty-one inches. December alone saw a fresh sixty inches fall, followed by another sixty inches in January.[2] All these storms paled in comparison to what came at the end

---

1 "Blizzard of 1977," *Wikipedia*, https://en.wikipedia.org/wiki/Blizzard_of_1977.
2 Ibid.

of January, though, when three days straight of thirty- to sixty-mile-per-hour winds gathered all the packed snow from Lake Erie and dumped it on Buffalo and the surrounding area. Drifts grew as high as twenty-five feet tall, and the national guard was called in to help the completely overwhelmed regular snow removal crews.[3]

The blizzard forced industries and schools to curtail activities and, in some cases, close—except for my college. Not that it mattered to me anyway, since I didn't go to class. I just watched the snow drifts pile up higher than my second-story window and thought death might be my only way out.

After the blizzard, the storm of failing out of college stared me in the face. The snow drifts blocked most of the view from my second-floor dorm window, but they couldn't block out my horrible grades. My first semester grade report read: C in volleyball, D in zoology, F in chemistry, F in calculus. Not including volleyball, I had a 0.33 GPA, not even 1.0 (a 4.0 is what most college students try for). I thought that not only had I failed, but that I was a failure. The sun stopped shining outside, but it had stopped shining within me a long time ago. What small light I did have seemed even darker.

I felt like I was living in a nightmare where I'd wake up in the dream only to find I was still asleep. Day or night, the darkness prevailed. Sadness and hopelessness filled my heart. I considered myself in the land of the living dead. Only weed and alcohol eased my pain.

---

3 Ibid.

THE DARKNESS BEFORE DAWN

Of course, the blizzard coincided with the energy crisis, so even as we endured inescapable snow and cold, the power grid flickered unpredictably. As the heat faltered, I sat frozen in my dorm room, chilling my bones by the frosted window. The depths of my despair convinced me that death would end it all. *No one cares about me anyway, so who would even notice?* I reasoned.

The pain I felt inside cut far deeper than the forty-mile-per-hour winds and minus-fifty-degree wind chill. I felt unspeakably lonely and drained, in a blank state of mind and soul that I can't even describe. This sense of feeling drained wasn't like feeling empty; it was laced with a greater sense of loss than mere emptiness, and it weighed so incredibly much. It seemed only suicide would end the fatigue of carrying around this pain year after year, stored deep inside of me.

Yes, I thought, *suicide will end this misery and suffering. This is a different kind of hell than the heated turmoil of New York City. This is a frozen hell with no sun—just snow, ice, wind, and the walking dead.*

A Light and a Future

In my darkest hour, something beyond reason interrupted me as I planned my death—I felt a warm touch on my shoulder. I felt it physically. Despite the pervasive cold in my room, my body felt warm all over. Then I heard an almost audible voice telling me, "Everything will be okay. Just hang in there." Again I heard, "Just hang in there." An increased warmth came over me, then a peaceful feeling of love and comfort. Even though I didn't know for sure, it felt like those comforting words were from my mom.

Years later, I look back with the realization that I was going from one trauma to the next, but the blizzard made time stand still. It made the pain of life and all the trauma up to that point hang in the frozen air like a movie put on pause. The positive spin on it now is my gratitude for the strength these traumas bestowed upon me. They inspired me to be a man of compassion who never assumes I understand what people are going through. They instilled in me a deep trust that God was there for me, contrary to the chaos all around me.

This was a turning point for me. My experience during that blizzard of despair helped me realize what should have been obvious, that my dysfunctional behaviors were not serving me well. I started to question everything I had ever thought to be true, which, at that time in life, meant questioning whether I really was alone. My mantra had been "I can only count on myself," yet there I was—my loneliness had been beautifully violated and my depression had been wonderfully invaded.

Even my cold had been warmed, and all of it happened without any invitation or expectation. I had cried out to God to save my mother and He didn't, and I had long since stopped crying out to God for myself, yet He did save me. It certainly didn't answer any questions for me, but it did make me question what I thought was true.

As the snow slowly melted that May of 1977, I went behind my dorm and discovered railroad tracks. It seemed odd to me

THE DARKNESS BEFORE DAWN

that I hadn't noticed the tracks or the train before, but this thought drifted away as I heard the train approaching. I watched as the train headed west, slowly passing me by.

The sun broke through the clouds, peaking out at sunset almost as if to say hello. Then, from somewhere I couldn't remember, the phrase "Go west, young man" began repeating in my mind. Historically, this was a phrase that represented the hope of escaping into a new life, and, even though college was a better alternative than the city, I was not getting anywhere in that direction.

This idea of going west was my only inspiration, so I went to the library and researched the American West. I found that the westward expansion of the 1800s gave the opportunity for anyone willing to work hard to succeed. I was able and willing to work hard, so I thought maybe it could work for me as well.

This new idea stirred within me hope for freedom and a vision for a new way of life.

Since the city wasn't an option and college wasn't working, I needed a different plan, and going west sounded like a new beginning. Maybe it would even be a place where I could find answers for some of the questions beginning to swirl in my mind.

How I would pay for it, I didn't know. Where I would go, I also didn't know. I only knew there had to be a better place somewhere on earth.

What I did know, as much as I hated it, was that this new plan would require me to work one more summer in New York City. I would just have to navigate that place a little longer. Just three more months there would mean freedom from New York and hope that something better awaited me out West. My hope and vision became synonymous with the railroad tracks behind my dorm room, where the train always headed from east to west, reinforcing the phrase "Go west, young man."

Son of Sam

Why was it that every time I thought I had hope, some new twist would happen to jab the knife of fear deeper? This time, I came back from college just in time to find out that a number of murders and attacks that had occurred over the past year were all connected, and the perpetrator was still on the loose. In other words, New York didn't just have gangs, mobs, muggers, riots, and protests; New York also now had a serial killer.

THE DARKNESS BEFORE DAWN

Thankfully, I didn't fit the typical description of the victims—female with long, wavy brunette hair, or with their significant other often sitting with them in a car—but that didn't change the new level of fear penetrating the atmosphere of the city. If you've never lived in a city where a serial killer is on the loose, let me tell you, everyone in the city is thinking about them, and not only when the killer has just attacked again.

This killer, who named himself the Son of Sam, caused women to cut their hair short, dye it blond, or simply wear a wig. Parents forced their children to stay in groups. Couples took care to avoid sitting for long in a parked car, as that's where many of the attacks happened. These actions show the psychological impact of having the questions hanging over you: When will the next attack come? Who's next? Will it be someone I know? Will it be me?

Working my old job again, I didn't have the luxury of staying away from Queens, where most of the attacks happened. I had to travel everywhere in town, never knowing what trouble I might meet. It didn't help that the press media dutifully kept the story in front of everyone in the city all summer long.

At least I still had my favorite pizza—Ray's. The owner, Ralph Cuomo, had gone to prison for a few years after being caught with $25 million worth of heroin in his trunk, but he was back now, and his pizza was still as good as ever. I didn't know at the time that heroin was still his biggest business. All I knew was that his pizza was my one consistent comfort in the city, and it was about to become more important than ever as yet another crisis was about to hit.

RACE TO THE SKY

One of New York's Darkest Hours

Aside from Ray's Pizza, one of the few things I could do to escape the pain of working in New York City was to go to a movie for a couple of hours. I often had nothing else to do, but I couldn't know what awaited me one particular hot summer night when I left the theater.

Walking out of the cinema, I was startled to find everything to the right of me was lit up, while everything to the left was pitch dark, including all of New York City. It was a sight and night I would never forget, but I wouldn't understand what had happened until the next day.

I was near my goal. Soon I would be free. I had bought a used Volkswagen Bug and was ready to drive away in it. I only needed another six weeks of pay to have the one thousand dollars I had calculated I would need to get me, my Bug, and my duffle bag as far away from New York as I could drive.

With that hope, I drove off to the construction company and stopped for a bagel. That's when I saw the headline: "24 HOURS OF TERROR." I bought the newspaper and went to work. My bosses had mercy on me that day and didn't send me into the city. Instead, I worked in the basement of the construction company, where I pored over the paper I'd bought.

I quickly found out that lightning had struck a power substation, leading to a power outage in all five city boroughs. Looting and arson ensued. Well over a thousand stores reported loss as people walked through the streets with their stolen goods, unhindered. Nearly four thousand people were arrested that night as the widespread crime grew uncontrollable.[4]

Interestingly, an even larger blackout had happened twelve years previously, with none of the same results. This showed just how much New York had lost itself so completely. It also confirmed to me more than ever that I needed to get out.

A Year of Blur

My plan was to leave by August 15 with enough money to get to the West Coast and still have a few hundred bucks to get a place. As that date drew near, however, I didn't have the money to leave, so instead I decided to try college again, work one more summer, and leave on August 15, 1978. Every day of that year was painful agony, but the vision of leaving got closer and closer.

Like every other time in my life, I was afraid. What would this new frontier look like? While New York City celebrated being a melting pot of diversity, it didn't pay much attention to the world beyond the city limits, so I had no idea what the broader world might be like, except for what I'd experienced during my year at college. I knew no one would be there for me in that new place, but no one had been there for me where I was either. I was poor, but my work ethic was good. I also believed my experience of working in the worst parts of New York City

---

4 "New York City blackout of 1977," *Wikipedia*, https://en.wikipedia.org/wiki/New_York_City_blackout_of_1977.

had prepared me for the Wild West. I figured it couldn't possibly be any worse than the Big Rotten Apple.

Would I miss getting drunk at the local dive bar that smelled like piss? Or would I miss the slices of hot pizza that would burn the roof of my mouth at three a.m.? Since I was too drunk and high to notice how hot the pizza was, in the morning I would have blisters on the roof of my mouth that barely allowed me to swallow.

I drank a lot of beer in those days, smoked pot and cigarettes, and had sex whenever and wherever I could (except for with prostitutes). Those were all things I could probably find wherever I went, so I most likely wouldn't miss those, though I would need to find new people to do all that with.

Would I miss the crowds, beeping horns, weather, muggings, fast-paced life, or people's rudeness? Would I miss the secret New Yorker's handshake of not doing anything to help another while they were being mugged? Would I miss homeless people with filth in their pants passed out drunk in the subways or the old ladies sleeping on the sidewalk? Would I miss not finding a parking spot or smelling people's sweat on a hot, muggy New York City day when you could taste the grime of the streets and subways? Would I miss this concrete jungle where you couldn't even see the sun by day, let alone the stars by night? Would I miss working in a constant state of fear in God-forsaken neighborhoods?

No, I was convinced I would not miss one thing about that place except maybe Ray's Pizza.

As the new planned day of departure drew near, my fear of

THE DARKNESS BEFORE DAWN

the unknown continued to be overpowered by the fear of staying. I knew moving out of New York was the best thing for my sanity, so I moved up the big day of leaving to August 7. That last week in the city, it rained every day. I was in a perpetual state of anticipation and excitement to the point of it being almost unbearable, and the weather made me want to leave all the more. What a gloomy, depressing, cloudy week! I couldn't stand being there another minute.

At six a.m. on the morning of August 7, I got into my VW Bug. Lightning and thunder came marching over me as I started up the car. The rain raged with fury, then a flash of forked lightning chased across the sky and a great clap of thunder shook my Bug as I neared the Long Island Expressway. The wind and rain came on so heavy that my windshield wipers couldn't keep up.

Goodbye, New York, I thought, but then skidding on my bald tires, I feared whether I would even make it out of the city.

I went to my old friend, music, for comfort. Only my favorite band could fit this moment—Steely Dan. I turned the volume up on "Bad Sneakers," a hopeless song with a happy tune. The lyrics rhythmically beat out themes of loneliness, the feeling of going crazy, and the belief that it's foolish to try to make anything out of life, but the music was upbeat and chipper. I could relate to all of that. Just as the song said, I thought New York City would drive me insane, so I laughed at the rain that felt like one last try by the city to keep me in its captivity—a captivity deeper than geography, pervading into what I thought life could be like.

Steely Dan comforted my fears as I crept from the Long

RACE TO THE SKY

Island Expressway to the Cross Island Parkway to the Cross Bronx Expressway, which had the worst congestion in the nation. Suddenly my Bug came to a halt. All I could see was traffic everywhere, with graffiti-stained concrete as a backdrop.

I reflected on the countless hours of my life stuck in traffic leaving or heading into New York City. There was always traffic, always bumper to bumper, and even taking the back streets didn't help. An hour went by before I saw the sign for the George Washington Bridge. I grit my teeth as the horns blared. Freedom and peace were close but not close enough. Not moving, I let my mind drift as I stared at the sign for Yankee Stadium, which I could see by looking over my left shoulder.

Great Yankee legends.

THE DARKNESS BEFORE DAWN

It reminded me of the great Yankee legends, almost like relatives from the Yankee family. Babe Ruth, Joe DiMaggio, and Yogi Berra to name a few. I had fallen hard for the Yankees the very first time I saw Mickey Mantle play at Yankee Stadium when I was young, and leaving them, the only family I knew, grieved me.

It was the team of 1977 that I would miss the most. Watching the feuds between Billy Martin, Reggie Jackson, and George Steinbrenner was like a circus, with their larger-than-life personalities and egos leading them to constantly bicker with each other. Having them all on the same team made for good fun and an endless blaze of spellbinding publicity. From Billy and Reggie fighting in the dugout during a game to their winning the World Series, they were the most exciting team in baseball. They were the closest thing I had to family. *Yes*, I thought, *I will miss the Yankees.*

A blaring horn broke me from my thoughts. As I glared into my rearview mirror, I could see the truck driver gesture out the window, giving me the Bronx salute—the middle finger—as he hung his head out the window and cussed me out. I cussed him right back in my thoughts as I rushed the clutch, jerking my way forward.

When I finally inched my way onto the George Washington Bridge, excitement replaced my anger at the truck driver and the sense of loss at leaving the Yankees. Halfway across the bridge, I looked back at Yankee Stadium, then at the Hudson River, and then I was across.

I remembered the story about my grandpa working on this

very bridge, facing danger and death every day just to provide for his family in a hard, new world. Now I was following in his footsteps, leaving the only home I knew to find opportunity somewhere else. Like my grandpa, I knew it would take hard work, and I was willing to do it. He had literally paved my way to freedom, setting the example for me to follow and building the bridge on which I would escape. He sang his song, and now I went out, hoping to rediscover mine.

The Washington Bridge spanning the Hudson River.

Chapter Six

I THOUGHT
I WAS ALIVE

My trip to California reminded me of *The Grapes of Wrath*. I had read that in my high school English class, and, like me, the family in the story was running for their lives to California. They ran from the Great Depression and the Dust Bowl, while I ran from all the terrors of New York City, but we both ran, hoping California would solve our problems.

In some way, their story helped inspire me even though it didn't end well. Their perseverance and what they did to survive encouraged me despite how I was petrified inside. I didn't realize my mind was trapped in a prison called The Big Apple, and I couldn't know for sure that I was being released from that prison. All I knew was I was leaving that world—the struggles of the working-class, blue-collar job in the big city, hoping to find a new life and future by going to college in California.

As each mile passed, I dreamed of what my new life might look like. My dream was to get away, and the closer I got to Santa Barbara, the more my daydreams involved a new way of life and a place where I could find myself and be a great person—someone like those I saw on the big screen.

Yes, like the heroes I witnessed in the movies, I was broken, but there was redemption for a new way of life somewhere deep in my soul. I'm sure I didn't need California specifically to make all this happen, but I was now California dreaming, and the most important thing was it wasn't New York City. Thankfully, unlike the Joads in *The Grapes of Wrath*, California greeted me with open arms and a new hope of a better life than I had thus far experienced.

My first day in Santa Barbara began with sunshine and the Pacific Ocean gently splashing on the shoreline. With the beach on one side and picturesque mountains, like ones I'd seen in movies, on the other, I connected with this place. It seemed to have a spiritual connection to my soul for me to change and transform my life, even though I wasn't consciously aware of it. Between the ocean and mountains were palm-tree-lined streets paved in places with red bricks. The commercial main street was filled with shops, boutiques, art galleries, restaurants, and bars. Everything looked like life to me, so different and far removed from the smokestacks spewing out air pollution, graffiti-stained subways, dirty buildings, crime-filled shops, and the fear that the streets of New York City emanated. Being in Santa Barbara was like breathing clean air for the first time in my life, and it gave me hope that maybe life could be different.

Santa Barbara coast.

My journey to find my soul song began with hiking back into nature, starting with my VW Bug winding along gorgeous mountain ridges that had incredible vistas over the city and sea the entire way. This jaw-dropping scenery, combined with magical sunsets, made me feel at times that perhaps heaven might exist here on earth.

Since the temperatures were in the sixties to eighties year-round, it always felt like spring or summer. Both of the colleges

I initially attended were situated on the ocean, and this was an enormous uplift to my spirit. This new environment provided a way for me to begin a new chapter of my journey, and my soul began to awaken.

Reality set in the next morning when I reached into my pocket, which confirmed that I had about $700 left. With that in my pocket, a VW Bug, and one duffel bag of clothes, I needed a room and a job. I understood that $700 wouldn't last long. It wasn't hard finding minimum-wage jobs, but I got bored easily and wound up jumping from one to the other.

At one job, I was doing construction and noticed a need for a painter. I knew this was the best money-earning opportunity I would find at the time and told one of the guys that I could do it for $10 an hour. With the laws at the time, and because I was paid cash, I was able to keep everything I earned without needing to pay taxes on it. Also, that one job led to more jobs after I posted a note on the school bulletin board that read "Richie's Painting: Quality painting at an affordable price."

Now I was bidding jobs, so instead of receiving an hourly wage while working for someone else, I was controlling my costs and earning an average of $20 an hour. In some cases I earned even more, depending on the height of the building. (Keep in mind that in 1978 in the United States minimum wage was only $2.65 an hour.)

This beginning taught me how to talk my way into one job after another. With a surfboard rack on my VW, I would strap on my ladder and put my brushes, pans, and rollers in my small backseat. My business cards included a caricature of a painter running across the card with a bucket in one hand and a brush in another. This depicted my state of mind as I was running from one job to the next, worried I wouldn't have enough money to pay for tuition and food.

Eventually, I wound up even painting part of the school I was attending. The catch was I had to do it at night when there were no classes, so I went to school by day and painted at night, getting about three hours of sleep per night. It didn't bother me, though, since I felt like I had it better than most people still stuck in New York City.

Year one went by, then year two, and I had to choose between sports and work. I decided to work part time and apply myself to playing Lacrosse in college. I could afford it for one semester, as I had saved $3,600. In addition, I had converted a two-bedroom house into a six-bedroom house, owned by the Del Monte heirs.

It was a real animal house, with petitions going around the neighborhood to get us kicked out. With only guys living there, we had mushrooms growing in the bathroom and rats that staggered in and out with an attitude after drinking the residue from beer bottles in the backyard. Besides the many parties, I had half my team living there, so it was one of the craziest, most insane, carefree, and fun times of my life.

Renting out converted closets as bedrooms at a whopping $150 per month, I didn't have to pay out of pocket for rent each month. In fact, I was up a couple of hundred at the end of each month. This seemed like I had it made. With no rent and a little extra every month, I was living large just like the rats. There was a real freedom in having some of these experiences. For the most part, it was clean fun, but what really made it special was the comradery. Being part of an undefeated team, and with many of us living together, I finally had a sense of belonging to something that felt like it mattered, even if it was for just a short time.

Leaving School

By 1981 I was burned out from both working and going to school, so I had to drop one or the other. I picked school. Sure, school was great; UC Santa Barbara was voted the number-one party school by *Playboy* magazine that year. I also won MVP for defense on our undefeated team. But for me it wasn't about the diploma; it was about whether I achieved what I wanted to accomplish. My attitude was that I was not going to march to society's drumbeat, rather I was going to take the road less traveled. I dropped out of school after that championship year, planning to open a restaurant and then finish my degree a few years later at another college.

Oh boy, what a journey that turned out to be! Having been voted MVP, I had confidence that I hadn't felt in a long time. Not a lot, but some, and to a person starved of confidence it was significant. I also had a beautiful girlfriend who was a smart career woman and graduated college with honors, and I was thinking about marriage.

We were having the time of our lives. We spent many weekends driving her convertible VW Bug to great places throughout

California. She was a fun, vivacious California girl with long blonde hair and sparkling blue eyes. I was living the dream, with my rent-free home in Santa Barbara, my California-girl girlfriend, and no real cares in the world.

Then one day the dream stopped. We got news that would change our lives: my girlfriend was pregnant. Next to my mom's death, this turned out to be one of the most emotionally challenging events thus far in my life. Being raised Catholic, an abortion was out of the question, so I really wanted her to have the baby, but that wasn't an option in her mind. She knew how radically becoming parents would change our lives, and wasn't willing to make those changes.

After numerous discussions, her decision was to abort our child and she wanted my full support. Horribly torn, I chose to support her, for us to go through it together. It wasn't until later in life that I would find out the full significance of our choice, but even in the moment there was no doubt it was truly significant.

I felt responsible for the abortion, and even though it wasn't my final decision or what I wanted, I believed it was a living baby and felt crushed by guilt. Doubts swam through my thoughts. Maybe my girlfriend felt I wasn't good enough? Maybe she didn't really love me? Maybe she didn't want to keep the baby because she thought I didn't do well enough in college?

Like everything else in life, I didn't know how to handle this difficult time, so I did the only thing I did know how to do: I stuffed it and kept running. No, I didn't run from my girlfriend; we stuck together despite going through this. I simply ran from the pain and pretended it wasn't there, just like I always did. *Keep running, kid. Never look back, and you might outrun the phantom*—at least so I thought.

Lessons in Business

By this time, painting had become monotonous, so I started working at one of the best pizza places in town. I liked pizza and it represented comfort for me, reminding me of Ray's. After three months, I thought I knew it all and opened my own pizza restaurant. My attitude and way of thinking then supported a bumper sticker I once saw: "Hire a 23-year-old while they still know everything."

Introducing a New York-style pizza restaurant (hold the heroin) into Santa Barbara was a hit. What I didn't know in business I soon learned, as I made every mistake possible, especially when it came to the lease. I was just thankful that they would lease the shop to me, but since I was successful, they kept raising the rent and my overhead became very high. This meant that although sales were good, overall profit wasn't. I considered this another lesson of life, but at least I learned from it—just not in time to keep me from another mistake.

I thought that if one restaurant was doing well in sales but not profits, then I needed to open another one. I should have known better from simple common sense, but I opened a breakfast shop next to the pizza place, using the same kitchen for both places. During the day I ran the breakfast place and at night I ran the pizza place, driven by my fear of failure.

Working very hard became a pattern for me, because failure was never an option since it meant being like the people living on the streets of New York City. The phantoms of those homeless people chased me everywhere I went, always right behind breathing down my neck. My difficulties in school and the feeling of not being smart made me believe I would have to outwork others to get ahead. I thought if I kept running from that phantom, I would eventually outrun it and be free.

Burnout, Bugs, and Real Estate

In another repeating pattern, by 1984 I had burned out from working double duty at the two restaurants. I hadn't learned yet that fear is a slave driver that can find you anywhere and follow you no matter how far you run. In all my hard work, I never escaped fear; I only numbed it by tricking myself into thinking I was doing something about it. When working hard didn't do that, I numbed it by running headlong after the hippie lifestyle.

I sold both restaurants, bought a VW bus with a peace sign in the back, and grew my hair long. I thought, *Ah, the hippie life! Free and easy!* With my new girlfriend I drove around the country looking for the next utopia. Instead, I found a 110-degree heatwave in the Midwest with heat wafting off the pavement. The fans I had installed in the front of the bus could only blow hot air on us, so with no air conditioning it was a brutal trip. I did discover the Northwest on that trip, though. I loved what I saw but decided to keep traveling.

Landing in Florida, I discovered that VW convertibles were

cheap. I did not, however, find utopia, so a year later I was back in Santa Barbara. Even so, this wasn't all a loss for me, because discovering where to buy cheap VW convertibles turned into a business opportunity. I could buy a Bug for $1,600 and sell it for $4,000. So I would take a one-week vacation, find a VW Bug convertible in Florida, buy it, and drive it across the country. After gas and some clean-up, I would make a $2,000 profit, in addition to getting a free vacation.

With this and my remaining money from the sale of the restaurants, I was able to buy my first house in Santa Barbara for a $105,000, putting $5,000 down while the owners carried the note for the rest. That house today is worth $1 million, but unfortunately I sold it three years later for $220,000. Still, to me at the time, this was a small fortune.

You Can Run But You Can't Hide

It was now 1985 and things were going great. I had bought my way back into the restaurant business, was running a successful Italian restaurant, and my real estate investments were growing, with houses purchased in Santa Barbara. There was just one problem (at least so I thought): my new girlfriend was pregnant. Thankfully, my problem wasn't that she wanted an abortion. This time, the problem was that she didn't want an abortion, which meant facing all the choices that come with having a child. The most difficult part of that was that we weren't married. These days, having a child out of wedlock may not seem like a big a deal, but in those days it was huge.

I THOUGHT I WAS ALIVE

I thought to myself, *Hey, no big deal. I can still raise my child with my girlfriend while living a single life with no responsibilities. I can make it work.* I still didn't know my song, and I was still running from any emotions. I couldn't stop to reflect on these sorts of things and didn't know I needed to. It was the old defense mechanism I'd learned while my mom was dying from cancer.

My girlfriend and I had gone over this already. I was convinced that my decision to not get married and instead pursue the bachelor life was the best thing for me. Things were in motion to keep it all that way, as my girlfriend and child lived on the other side of a duplex from me. I owned it and she rented from me. But a funny thing happened when I arrived home from the restaurant one day.

Upon my opening the sliding door leading to the backyard full of fruit trees, a breeze swept through the branches. It was different than most breezes, as it touched me in a way that seemed to communicate with my soul. As this warm, gentle breeze landed on my being, I dropped my head into my hands. My life up to that point flashed before me.

Suddenly an invisible presence flooded over me, engulfing me, flowing around me, through me, running down, then back up, then down again, like I was being immersed in love inside and out. I was stunned from the first moment, completely overwhelmed, but it kept getting stronger. The presence was so encompassing that I felt like I was in a different dimension. I was at complete peace from head to toe. More than that, I felt that I was loved and cleansed in such a way that I could see clearly from a perspective that was beyond this world.

That's when I knew in the depths of my being that this was God's Holy Spirit, that this incredible love was inseparable from His Spirit. It was not earthly love, and it was not human love. It was the purest unconditional form of love. I knew then beyond doubt that God's nature is love and there was no question that I was loved and was being cradled in His arms.

I had run from God for so long, questioning and doubting whether He even existed. I had been convinced that if He did exist, He was cold and distant. He didn't know my name and number and he certainly didn't hear my prayers. My life-saving experience in Buffalo had cracked that way of thinking, but this encounter wedged the crack wide open. I still had a long way to go (and still do), but this was the moment I became convinced of God's love. This was the moment I got saved and knew I needed to change.

It became clear that my old way of thinking was not in alignment with God's plan for my life. In fact, all my thoughts did a 180-degree turn. Everything I had thought was wrong, and it was now clear that marrying my girlfriend and being a responsible father was the right path to be on. With this new conviction, feeling, and perspective, I went next door and asked my girlfriend to forgive me and if she would marry me. She accepted and we became reunited in a new journey with each other and with God.

Why did this supernatural experience happen to me? Was it because of some kind of repentance on my part? No, it was purely God's love and mercy for me. It was a depth of love that cannot be explained in human terms, just as a spiritual experience cannot be fully explained in the natural. As I was consumed by

God's love, there was no resistance, just acceptance and a feeling of deep love. Now I had no fear of getting married, no self-righteousness, no more pride, no more ego, no more denial of the truth, and no more excuses that it was other people's fault. Yes, I had come to the end of myself, and instead of it being painful and hard, it was peaceful and comforting. It was also liberating to feel God's love embrace me.

The Spirit of God doesn't produce a spirit of fear; God's perfect love casts out all fear (1 John 4:17–18). I was not scared or nervous in the slightest. It wasn't like something taking over my body. In actuality, this love from God felt very familiar. Even though nothing like this had ever happened to me before, I was totally comfortable and at ease in His presence. God knew me and I knew I was completely accepted exactly the way I was. There was no performance necessary, no great feats to conquer, no feeling that I needed hide my true self. God knew the true me; He made my blueprint; and He knew my hopes, dreams, and gifts for this world.

The perceived failures and fears no longer mattered; all I felt was love to the very core of my being.

God Met Me

Just as incredible as this first encounter with God, was what happened shortly afterward. Having just become a born-again Christian, I was receiving counseling from the pastor at church. He knew nothing about my background, but an odd thing happened during one session with him.

About fifteen minutes into the session, he said, "I'm getting something from the heavenlies." In other words, God was giving him a message for me.

"What?" I asked.

"It's odd," he answered. "It's a little girl's voice." Then his voice changed to that of a little girl, and the voice spoke through him, "Daddy, I'm okay. I'm up in heaven and everything is fine up here. I look forward to meeting you, and I get to play with all the other boys and girls here. I love you very much, Daddy, and I am very happy." Then almost as if the pastor was coming out of a trance, he shook his head and said, "Wow. That has never happened to me before." He was sixty-five years old, so it had to have been a very unusual experience for him.

The truth is it was even more unusual for me, but I desperately needed it anyway. God knew I needed to hear that message because I had so much guilt about the abortion my college girlfriend had. I then told the pastor the entire story.

"That's incredible!" he said. "It makes perfect sense as to why this just happened."

We both went away from that session amazed at God's goodness and power because of the way He worked in my life that day. It was the first healing experience I would have from my past trauma, but not my last. The best was yet to come.

While I would still need to face all my other traumas one day, for the time being, the one challenge I still needed to overcome was smoking pot. I had been using pot to medicate my emotional pain for years. It was too much to quit on my own, so I prayed that God would take away the addiction.

I vowed to change my life and do the right thing, to get married and be the TV dad I thought I should be. I couldn't do it on my own, however, so I asked God to meet me halfway. If I would commit to living a godly life, would He please take the addiction away? I asked for this to happen from the day of my wedding going forward. It was the beginning step in my learning to trust God again. On that day, He took away my cravings for alcohol and pot, which had lasted for twenty years. It wasn't until my kids were in college that I started to drink beer and wine again.

Yes, this was a new beginning for me. My heart was open to God for the first time since I was eleven. I recognized that He had always been with me, but being with me was not the same as being welcome to work in me. While I had tasted a miraculous rebirth of trusting God and believing in Him, I had a long way to go before I would fully come to the end of myself, stop running, and allow God into my pain. Only facing a danger worse than any I faced in New York City would drive me to that final, desperate decision.

Chapter Seven

MY LAST GASP

When the 1980s began, I was scraping my way through college and finding my way in a world that was still new to me. Now, as the 1980s were nearing their end, I thought I was finally beginning to make headway. After my encounter with God's love, I married my wife in 1986. We had our first daughter soon after that, and not too much later added another little girl. I was now a husband and father of two.

These new responsibilities drove me after financial success more than ever. My restaurant and real estate investments were going wonderfully, which enabled me to keep buying more investment properties. In 1987 we built a fifteen-acre ranch in Santa Barbara (it eventually made the cover of some magazines).

Everything looked perfect, but inside I was still running. I had no sense of my purpose or my song; I only had the pressure to do more. Within me a perfect storm of complexes were all working together to drive me on. Go, go, go! Work, work, work! The phantom of fear was still there.

While I no longer lived with my alcoholic father, I still acted out the hero role. I gave and gave, never pausing long enough to realize that I also needed to receive. I saw only the need to care for others, to make sure my family's needs were met, so I had no regard for my own. I never even saw or thought of them. Any emotions that might remind me I had needs hadn't seen the light of day for decades. I had no idea that in order to truly love others well, I needed to love myself first.

My hero role, my fear of failure, my need to survive, and now the pressure of providing for a family kept me feeling like my back was against a wall. All my achievements gave me no comfort, no room to breathe, and no time to look inside to begin the healing process. If I keep running fast, I told myself, I may never have to look back into the depths of pain and trauma.

On the surface, my problem was that I would eventually burn out—again. But deeper, my problem was that I was living for the world's definition of success. I had bought the lies of worldly achievements—hook, line, and sinker. If I didn't have money, I was a failure. If I didn't have an amazing property, I was a failure. If I didn't have a growing income, I was a failure. If I didn't have great cars, I was a failure. Failure was never an option for me, but I didn't realize the emptiness of everything I was working so hard to gain.

I was stuck in a pattern, and sure enough, I did eventually burn myself out, just as I had before. Worse, the savings and loan crisis progressively grew during the entire time I was investing in real estate. This crisis was almost entirely related to real estate, and we took huge losses in 1989 and sold many of our properties.

I had thought that if I worked hard enough and ran fast enough, I would outrun my pain and fears. I thought that if I could be successful in the way the world measures success, then I would be able to breathe, confident and at peace. Now so much of the progress I had made toward those goals was crashing down around me, all while I overworked myself at my restaurant.

I finally decided to sell that too, and to leave Santa Barbara. Packing up my family, I headed for the Pacific Northwest. There was no way I could know that this move would require me to stare death square in the face—and ask myself, "Will I only count on myself, or will I finally trust God?"

But God had something in store for me that would help me jump off the hamster wheel of pursuing worldly success.

Yet Another Restaurant

I was the sole provider for my family, and I felt imprisoned by two realities. First, if I didn't work hard and produce money, my family would suffer. Second, I had no profession in which to make money. Sure, while going to college I was able to paint homes and do odd construction jobs while working in restaurants to get by, but I never had the confidence or training in any field that would make the money necessary to provide for three people plus myself.

On my own I had survived, since I lived in an animal house in college, subsisting on less than $300 per month. But I wanted to be an all-American dad—like the dads I'd seen on TV, not the dad I grew up with—so what else could I do? I had to step up, provide, and be the dad I never had.

An old Pizza Hut had gone out of business, and I was able to obtain a lease and open an Italian restaurant. Soon I discovered that my decision became a whole new type of prison sentence of working sixteen-hour days six days a week, with another half-day on Sundays. Owning and running a restaurant may sound romantic, but I had no passion for it and, frankly, I hated it. Having no budget to hire help made it an unbearable grind. I did it strictly out of fear that I wouldn't have the money I needed to provide for my wife and children. The only thing enjoyable was the food, since my recipes were amazing.

For seven years I worked as hard as I could, desperately trying to escape from owning a restaurant. There were no buyers and there was no bridge to transition into a new profession. I needed the weekly profits to survive and provide. I looked for ways out, but there were none to find. Finally, an offer came for the restaurant and it sold. I was finally free, or so I thought.

An Offer I Couldn't Refuse

It was a cold Pacific Northwest night, misty and dark. Watching the dagger before my eyes, I could see stains of human blood glimmering from the glow of the neon light flashing in

MY LAST GASP

the window. The man with the eight-inch knife was frightening enough, but it was worse knowing it was inches from my neck and he had killed many people before me. I was supposed to be next, but why me?

My life was about to end, the knife being waived by my throat getting closer and closer. The Mafia hitman kept telling me he was going to kill me, recounting the many executions he had done before and pointing to the blood-stained dagger.

My mind danced in a panic of one-second intervals. *What about my life and family? I have a wife and two kids to provide for. What if I try to run?* I knew there was no way out. *How can I be in this situation? I'm going to die.* The phantom had finally caught me, and fear consumed my being.

A few days prior to this, I was simply trying to sell my restaurant and thought I had an interested buyer. Now I was finding out the buyer was faking his interest. He was a Mafia hitman, and the only offer he was going to give me was a Godfather-like "offer I couldn't refuse." In other words, he was going to kill me and take my restaurant. I couldn't believe this was real, but the neon light illuminating the hulking, knife-wielding monster in front of me proved otherwise.

My life savings was in my latest restaurant. Except I had moved here for the very purpose of being free from the restaurant business, so how did I get here? Was it the phantom of fear, or was it simply not knowing another way to earn a living? Or was it a lack of confidence in my ability, or was it not having a real understanding that God was really with me on this journey called life?

What About God?

So there I was, staring back at a three-hundred-pound killer as he regaled me with stories of his previous murders. I knew I was too young to die, that I had not yet accomplished my soul's purpose.

As I looked into my would-be murderer's eyes, I could see only pure evil—only hate, only an obsession to kill. Staring deeper, I could see the window into his soul. It was a deep, dark pool of evil, void of anything good. In this endless black abyss was only hatred and a demon seething to kill. It was as if I stopped hearing the man's voice and instead could hear the demon's, speaking all the promises of how he was going to kill me. The more fearful I became, the more the demon seemed to grow stronger.

Okay, I said to myself, *no way out. Defeat. Surrender. I'm dead.* The thought lingered in my mind—death—and the question of what was next. *Oh. God! God is next! That's right! What about God? Is He real? Is He fact or fiction?*

Up to that moment I was in a complete state of fear. I could see and feel the presence of demonic evil. Suddenly my mind thought of Dante's description of hell, a place of unending torture and violent pain for all evil creatures, just like the one staring right at me. Thinking of this, I knew it would be the demons' fate but not mine, and inner peace came over me. I began to hope in God.

Then a Scripture verse came to mind: "If God is for us, who can be against us?" (Romans 8:31 NIV). In a peaceful voice I said, "Sure, you want to kill me. I get it." Then looking into his eyes directly at the demons, I added, "Know this: You cannot kill me unless God gives you permission to kill me. Let me grab something off my desk and show it to you."

The mobster now sat at a table in shock. I had no fear and felt I was taking control of my own death. After grabbing a Bible off my desk, I quickly made my way back to him. The demons were now seething pure hatred. Saliva was building up in the corners of my attacker's mouth, and his breathing intensified. It seemed at any moment he was going lunge over the table and plunge his dagger into my throat.

What surprised me was how calm and peaceful I felt in this moment of sure death. I took one last look at him and then looked down at my closed Bible on the table. I had resolved at that moment that either God is real or He is not. I decided that if He knew the number of hairs on my head, had created the earth and all the things in it, and He wanted me to die, then I would, but if He wanted me to live and fulfill my purpose, then I would. The only question hanging in my mind in that moment was, *Will I choose to trust God again?*

With that thought, I randomly opened the Bible, not knowing where my finger would land. Then I calmly read what was in front of me. It happened to be the book of Revelation, and I randomly started reading at Revelation 19:20. I kept reading, but here are the highlights from those passages:

> But the beast was captured, and with it the false prophet who had performed the signs on its behalf. With these

signs he had deluded those who had received the mark of the beast and worshiped its image. The two of them were thrown alive into the fiery lake of burning sulfur. … The sea gave up the dead that were in it, and death and Hades gave up the dead that were in them, and each person was judged according to what they had done. Then death and Hades were thrown into the lake of fire. The lake of fire is the second death. … "But the cowardly, the unbelieving, the vile, the murderers, the sexually immoral, those who practice magic arts, the idolaters and all liars—they will be consigned to the fiery lake of burning sulfur. This is the second death." (Revelation 19:20; 20:13–14; 21:8)

As I was reading, I heard soft weeping at first, but then it increased. Looking up, I saw this vicious Mafia hit man crying like a baby. The gold chains around his neck swayed to the rhythm of the weeping as his head jerked with each sob. His pudgy, hairy hands covered his face as sweat and tears seeped between his fingers.

My Miracle Resurrection

Surprised by the sudden turn of events, I kept reading the Bible. I would occasionally stop and encourage him that he could change his life and that God would forgive him. "You don't have to kill people," I said. "You can change your life now."

In between sobs he would gasp, "God will never forgive

me. I have killed so many people." He then pointed to the dried blood on his knife.

Eventually, he told me I was like a priest, so he began to confess his murders. I endured story after story of murder after murder—people he looked in the eyes as he shot, people who begged for their life before he killed them anyway, people the mob thought were ripping them off only to find out too late they hadn't, people with wives and kids.

Hours passed and the sun was now coming up. In hindsight, I don't remember how many murders he confessed to, but I heard about more than I could keep straight. Finally, I told him I would give him the restaurant on one condition—he had to change his life and heart. It was his chance to let Jesus forgive him for his sins. If he stopped killing people—*Like me, for starters*, I thought—he could have the restaurant for free. I thought it could change his life and maybe save mine.

The hitman kept weeping, insisting, "God cannot forgive me! I am evil and have done too many bad things."

"You're wrong," I said. "Jesus died for our sins."

Ultimately, this became an offer neither he nor I could refuse. I took him through prayers in the book of John and he gave his life over to God.

The rest is history. He took over the restaurant and began visiting churches to give his testimony of being a mob hitman who gave his life to Jesus. He also went on to do cooking demonstrations, changing his name to an exotic Italian name. As for me, I was broke but had found inner peace in the simple fact that I was alive. Praise God for love and mercy!

Frankly, it was a miracle that never would have happened if I didn't come to the end of myself. Death was inevitable. The change in the situation came when I decided to test whether God is real or not. I'd seen Him intervene in other moments, but never in something like this. It begged the question, would I trust Him again or keep running in my own strength? I had been running for decades, refusing to count on anyone but myself. I didn't believe I could count on anyone else, but being face-to-face with a Mafia hitman was beyond me. I couldn't count on myself to get out of that.

I finally chose to give God another chance. He had touched me in times of need throughout my life even though I wasn't following Him and didn't trust Him; He had still been there. Then, finally, when I knew I was going to either die that night or not, and it was completely in His hands which way things would go, I decided to trust Him again. I allowed God to step in, and that is when the miracle happened.

Getting Out of My Whale

My nightmare with the hitman brought me back to trusting God. However, it also meant that I had just racked up what felt like two, maybe three, perceived major failures in a row. First, I had failed to get a good offer on my Italian restaurant in Santa Barbara, selling it for a small down payment and a note. Then, I worked to buy a mortgage company but generated too many loans for one processor to process, which resulted in most loans not closing. Finally, I ran back to a life I already knew didn't

MY LAST GASP

work, only to be forced to give my entire investment away to keep a mobster from killing me.

I now found myself in a new town with two failed businesses, no money, no income, and a family that depended on me. Were these failures or learning lessons that would finally bring me to a place where I had to trust God? In fact, all of my perceived failures were really lessons I had to learn the hard way in order to get to that place of trusting God once again.

The one thing my dad helped me believe was that I could do anything, and since I'd survived growing up in a negative environment, I was determined not to fail and repeat what he did to my family. No matter how hard it would be, I would not abandon my wife and children. I would keep battling, even though I could see it was literally killing my heart and soul.

However, despite this determination and God's intervention to save my life, after all the perceived failures I'd stacked together, I was done. I had come to the utter end of myself. I had always been a positive person for whom failure was not an option, so when I began to stay in bed for days on end, it was frightening for both my family and me. As I lay in bed, I said, "God, if you're not going to use me, then you might as well kill me." I meant it and was not going to get out of bed until He killed me.

My wife panicked at this drastic change in my behavior, seeing that I had no desire to live or to even try to apply myself. After three days and nights, I was convinced my life would end since I refused to engage life at any level. As I lay there in bed, I distinctly remember taking what I considered to be my last breath, the final breath of surrendering to death, that was the last breath of myself being in control.

After an hour or so, in the distance I could hear the phone ring. My wife came in and said that a nonprofit organization was on the phone for me. They had heard what a great businessman I was and wanted to take me to lunch. (*Haha*, I would think when I later found that out, since I thought I was a complete failure.) Reluctantly I went to the meeting, thinking that if they only knew what had happened in my business life, they wouldn't be taking me to lunch.

As I sat there and listened to their offer of being a Director of Planning and Development, I thought of the biblical story of Jonah and the whale. He had run from God, just as I had, and finally spent three days inside a big fish God sent to put him in timeout so he could rethink his life. He finally stopped running and fulfilled his purpose.

The representatives from the nonprofit continued to tell me how excited they would be to have me grow their nonprofit and build a spiritual retreat. I kept thinking, *I can run just like Jonah, but I will be swallowed by the whale.* In my case, it was a three-hundred-pound human hitman whale. I could run but I couldn't hide.

Apparently, God's plan was to use me to help people instead of having me just make money. My soul purpose would begin once I trusted God again on my journey with Him. This was a journey I had never been on before, but I now saw no other option except to trust God. That last gasp of breath was meant to be my last before dying to myself, and it would be the last for that self-driven, fear-based survivor who could only count on himself. It was a long, hard fight, but it finally ended. I had to surrender being in control.

The first step was to surrender my mind to God. This changed not only what I thought, but what I put into my mind. My mind was saturated with fear from past trauma, and what we remember influences what we do. Proverbs 23:7 confirms this: "For as [a person] thinks in his heart, so is he" (NKJV). From my fears I took on false identities that made me believe I wasn't worthy of God's love, and from my TV role models I thought I could solve any problem in thirty minutes and control the outcome for a happy ending. But that's not the way real life turned out to be.

In giving God my mind, body, and will, I was going to fill my heart with love through a relationship with Him built on trust, walking with Him through whatever journey might come. I saw working with the nonprofit as the perfect way to try to live God's way and follow my soul's purpose. I thought it would be perfect for connecting with His love and becoming a shining light into the world.

Chapter Eight

HITTING MY STRIDE?

What I found, instead, is that Christians aren't perfect, and having a group of people who are all well-meaning and trying to serve others doesn't necessarily translate into smooth sailing without problems or conflict. This part of my journey with God into the nonprofit world was eye opening to say the least. Being naïve and expecting this world to be different from the rest of the world was very disappointing. It proved one sure thing—despite people's flaws and imperfections, God shows up anyway. I saw Him do miracles despite man's flaws. It became a learning experience like no other, that prepared me for a consulting business.

Taking the consulting business on the road to Seattle was not an easy thing to do. It was full of experiences (lessons) I perceived as failures, even though they were really just learning experiences. Setbacks and changes in plans served to provide me with a road map. The question was, would I follow it? Each wrong turn became a fork in the road that would lead to achieving my vision or goals if I followed. My mistakes fueled my passion and focused me to move forward, giving me the realization that if God was with me on the journey, then everything I went through was for a reason, which meant I could even learn to be thankful for the tough times. Although most of the time I never understood the trials and tribulations while I was experiencing them, I later would reflect on how they served a purpose in my growth. The main thing was to never give up.

At one point when I was on the verge of giving up, I went to a place called the Healing Rooms, started in 1914 by John G. Lake in Spokane, Washington. In the five years after he founded the rooms, there were one hundred thousand healings. Spokane became known not only as the healthiest city in America, but the healthiest city in the world.

In the 1990s, these rooms were reopened. At church I had heard about the Healing Rooms, but I didn't know the history of John G. Lake. I only knew that you could go there to get prayer. Since I was faced with not knowing where my next consulting job would be, I needed prayer, because, ultimately, I needed hope and faith that God was with me on this journey when there was no hope to be found in my natural circumstances.

Upon arrival at the Healing Rooms, I was greeted by a receptionist who told me to have a seat and wait for someone who would be with me shortly. After a brief wait, a couple came out and greeted my wife and me. We were then escorted to a small room where that couple asked our names and proceeded to pray.

After about fifteen minutes of prayer, the gentlemen started jumping up and down. "Hallelujah! Hallelujah! Hallelujah! A million dollars! A million dollars! A million dollars!" He kept shouting. Being raised Catholic, I thought he was nuts, but hey, it sounded good, so I went with it. When he was done praying, I asked him about his outburst. He simply said, "God is going to give you a million dollars."

I left wanting to believe that, but really didn't see any way it was going to happen. At this point I was commuting to Seattle to do consulting work, but making barely enough to pay the bills. I would mysteriously learn information for the next day's meetings, never knowing I would need that information at the time I learned it. It never dawned on me that I was being guided and directed. To me it was dumb luck. Failure seemed imminent, but I wanted to believe that word about a million dollars—and it was those words, blind faith, and maybe even a little dumb luck that would make it a reality.

Consulting and Economic Consternation

At this point in time I would travel six hours to Seattle, work three sixteen-hour days, then drive back the six hours. Leaving at three a.m. to make it there by nine a.m. week after week became difficult, as I almost fell asleep behind the wheel many times.

While I was consulting for nonprofits, for-profit businesses also approached me to consult for them, and of course I said yes. Frankly, the principles are the same, though I remember getting into many lively discussions with well-meaning board members of nonprofits who would say, "Why are you talking about generating profit to be self-sustaining on our products and services? After all, we're a nonprofit."

My issue with these statements was mainly that a nonprofit, in my opinion, had to not only seek gifts and grants, but also provide services and products that would generate revenue so the organization could sustain itself and provide more contribution toward its mission statement. Not all board members saw it that way, and this would lead to those lively discussions.

My for-profit consulting eventually led to doing consulting with Fortune 500 companies. At times this seemed surreal, as this was when information would come to me just before I needed it. When I received information unexpectedly, I didn't know why at the time, but within days it would become clear.

It was quite a journey in those days, as it was the mid-1990s and the dot-com boom was like the Wild West. We were raising large sums of money for startup companies that were based on hypothetical market share and, in many cases, they had no proven revenue model. No one knew how much of the overall economy these new tech companies would become, but every existing company wanted to make sure they owned a share of it. In other words, well-established companies were tripping over themselves to invest in startup tech companies that couldn't prove their plan for making money would work.

That's why that period was called the dot-com bubble,

HITTING MY STRIDE?

because anyone paying attention knew such a widespread blanket investment in an unproven industry was bound to eventually find more flops than successes. Along with some other economic dynamics, it was a perfect storm just waiting for the bubble to burst.

I knew the burst was coming and couldn't understand how so much money was being invested in startups. The whole movement was speculative and fad-based, which is no basis for sound investing. I couldn't understand how so many investors couldn't see that these companies had no real plan for how they would turn a profit, yet there they went, pouring money into internet startups in the hope that those companies would one day become profitable.

It was a reckless approach based on two things—fear and greed. These companies feared they would miss this incredible technology boom, and their greed to get money from this unstable boom led to them risking money on long shots.

A Promise Fulfilled

That's why I decided to buy an old-fashioned brick-and-mortar company that still made products for consumers. One year later I was especially relieved that I made this choice, because the bubble finally burst, and in spectacular fashion.

Even though I had predicted this, buying the company was not easy. I was consulting for this company, which was supplying products to consumers across the nation. We were working on a valuation plan for a buyout for this company, some issues came up with the sale of this company to another at the last minute, and I simply said I would buy it. The only problem was it would cost me $2.3 million, which was a lot more money in the late-1990s than it is even today. To me it seemed possible yet impossible at the same time. "Have faith," I told myself, "God is with you."

Using every skill and piece of knowledge I had at the time, I lined up every bank in the area and made copies of many documents for each bank. I submitted copies to well over fifteen banks. Each one came back with a resounding no.

The seller had given me only four months to raise the money and buy the company. Down to the end of my timeline, I was able to finally secure one approval letter from a bank for a million dollars. The remaining money I needed was negotiated, but what happened next was unheard of.

The day came for me to pick up my loan. In this case, the bank wrote me a check—for a million dollars! I was walking down the streets of Seattle with a one-million-dollar check in my hand! What was most amazing was that it was an unsecured check. That meant I had been given a one-million-dollar check that was unsecured against anything; it was the same as cash. My mind drifted back to the Healing Rooms as I bounced with jubilation down the sidewalks of Seattle. "A million dollars! A million dollars!" rang in my mind as I could almost hear those words again.

Purchasing this company became a new journey in the challenges of running an international company. Over nearly a twenty-year period, it grew from a mom-and-pop company to a

HITTING MY STRIDE?

large company. In addition to working this company, I had been buying and selling real estate since the age of twenty-four, which had many ups and downs, but the experience was irreplaceable.

At this point in life, I didn't understand why I enjoyed building houses and remodeling them, but maybe it was the generational blessings coming through from my grandpa. I strangely never had a fear of heights. Granted, I rarely went above three stories and, yes, I did fall off a few roofs along the way, but at least I wasn't a thousand feet up in the air on a skyscraper.

During all these business adventures, it seemed like I was learning and growing my business knowledge and acumen, however I felt like my soul was still in hiding. This shift came especially when I transitioned from the nonprofit world into the business world. In the nonprofit world, despite the disillusionment I faced, at least I was focused on helping people, while in the business world I was focused only on the bottom line. It wasn't until later that I learned the power of reflecting on life's experiences, which enabled me to blend both worlds together so I could help people while still being wise in a business sense.

I never stopped and looked back, however. I never stopped to congratulate myself on any of my advances or achievements. You see, I felt the demons and phantom of fear were always right behind me, chasing me relentlessly. I never realized I was in the top percentage of most people, being able to take the risk of having my own businesses.

The challenges and maneuvering required to navigate through the pitfalls of running an international company were immense. It was like walking the steel beams high up in a different kind of skyscraper—just as tenuous, threatening just as terrible of a fall at any moment. But it taught me that there are solutions to every problem and there is no situation too big for God.

It taught me the Continual Improvement Process, which tells you to reflect on past history so you can evaluate how to improve and be better at everything in life, which I did. My perceived failures became lessons that needed to be learned to grow and evolve no matter how hard they might have seemed at the time. This was huge for me, learning that my past was not just something to run from, but that it could be something to learn and grow from, if I was willing to look at it and meditate on it.

Lessons from Reflection

Learning to reflect on my past would eventually open the door to the deep healing I truly needed. It finally provided a past road map of what worked and what didn't work on my journey. Patterns were repeating themselves, good and bad; some were generational blessings and others were generational sins. These root-to-fruit patterns took years to identify, but the first step to change was to identify what the problems are.

The next step was to honestly look at them and break the patterns with a willingness to change. Some patterns that seemed insurmountable were eventually broken with divine intervention, but only when I cried out for help. Many negative patterns were revealed, which would be a lifelong journey to heal, but right away reflection began providing other benefits.

HITTING MY STRIDE?

First, it helped me destress. By purposely slowing down and taking time to think and reflect, I was able to release a lot of stress. This helped my brain function as God meant it to work, because stress begins to shut down our ability to think critically and logically, leaving us relying overly much on our emotions.

Second, taking time to reflect also enabled me to get a handle on how things were actually going. I could dig into the details and analyze the trending data both personally and in business. Imagine a situation where the amount of money you're bringing in is increasing but your profits are decreasing. Without taking the time to look into the situation, you might keep doing what you've been doing—after all, your revenue is increasing—but that would obviously be a mistake. You need to figure out why your profits are shrinking and address the issue before it takes you under. Never forget the simple yet sometimes overlooked principle of revenue up and expenses down equals profit.

Third, it turns out that we learn from reflection if we're willing to look at ourselves honestly. Problems in families and in business start at the top in most cases and then trickle down to the family members or employees. When we're constantly in motion, most of the experiences we have won't end up sticking with us, and they certainly won't get translated into any meaningful lessons. By taking the time to reflect on what happened, both good and bad, I was able to extract the underlying root causes and look for patterns. Not everything turned into some kind of eureka moment, but I certainly gained more from reflecting than when I didn't take time to do so.

After taking time to reflect, I began to ask questions. Had I been living my life out of fear? Had fear always been my motivating factor? Had that fear driven me to make money, and had that become something that was solely for my own gain? Was it still possible for me to move beyond fear? Could I possibly ever love myself? Would I ever connect back to my soul song?

In reflecting, I also realized that no matter how bad things were, I chose to believe good would happen despite the odds usually being against me (and at times looking downright impossible). It was during these quiet times of reflection that my soul began to connect with God and I was able to begin to hear the song my soul had wanted to sing my whole life. It was in these times that I realized my main purpose is to convey the message of God's love to people, whether in the nonprofit world or the business world.

In other words, my soul song was not static and could be used minute by minute, day by day, if I could stay connected with my soul, stay connected to God, and not succumb to fear. These gifts of connecting with people came from the little everyday things, not the grandiose monumental achievements I once thought I had to reach.

It was truly a revelation to me that our light can shine in any environment we're in if we remain connected to our soul and God. That connection can give us guidance and allow God to show up even when our life is on the line. My journey, and the lessons I learned from it, have been full of ups and downs, and challenges that go beyond description, but all of it prepared me to reconnect to my soul song. It also taught me how much God truly loves each and every one of us and how He wants us all to find Him and our soul song.

One particularly interesting thing that I realized from all the reflecting that went into writing this book is how many times I should have been killed but God supernaturally spared my life. Here are just two more of the many examples.

Don't Let the Dog Die

It was nine p.m. and I sat in the passenger seat of a Lexus sport car speeding down the 101 Freeway in California. I glanced over at the driver, a writer of one of the Beach Boys' songs, and I noticed he was locked in a trance-like state. Hoping to break the silence, I said, "Don, let's get something to eat."

No answer.

"Hey, Don. Let's get something to eat."

Still nothing.

Now I sat up, somewhat concerned. I glanced down at my Maltese puppy, Buddy, who was asleep, and then looked out my window as we sped by the car next to us. Then looking to the left, I saw that we were heading toward the concrete center divide. "Don! Don! Wake up!" I shouted.

Don was hunched over, unresponsive because of a seizure, but I thought he was dead behind the wheel. I knew I was near death too, because there was nothing we could do to avoid the high-speed collision with the median. Or was there? I didn't even have time to ask myself the question. I only had time to react, and then there was the car next to our car.

RACE TO THE SKY

I leaned over the center console, as there was not much room to maneuver. Grabbing the wheel, I guided the car back into the second lane from the center, wondering how this could possibly be happening. My heart was racing, and the sweat on my palms felt clammy and cold. Many thoughts rushed through my mind: *Turn off the engine. No, then the wheel will lock. Push his leg off the accelerator. No, his leg could press down harder on it. Think, think, think. What do I do? Okay, just steer until you think of something.* In the meantime, keep screaming Don's name hoping he will wake up. Nope, that's not working. Okay, now what?

Miles went by, and it seemed like hours on end, though the reality was it was only minutes. Finally, I put the right turn signal on and slowly guided the car into the righthand lane. Once there, I looked for an exit off the 101.

In the distance, I could see a long exit going uphill. Glancing down at my puppy, who was now awake, I saw him looking at me with eyes asking if there was something wrong. All I could think of was, *My wife will kill me if this dog dies.* With that thought, I sprang into action.

My head slammed into the roof as I threw my body over the console while my left leg groped for the brake. Missing the brake on the first try, I looked up, realizing the car was almost at the end of the offramp. *One last chance at the brake*, I thought, and I jerked my leg back toward the brake and put all my weight down on it.

Screeching wheels ensued as the smell of burning rubber filled the air. Turning the wheel to the side, the Lexus screeched to a stop.

HITTING MY STRIDE?

Sitting there in shock for a minute or two, I reached down and grabbed Buddy, holding him. I glanced over at my friend, who still looked like a dead man behind the wheel. I was dazed and confused. Was it luck that I walked away from that near accident with no injuries?

A year afterward, I still wondered how I had avoided getting killed. I concluded that it must not have been my time to die. *Maybe there is a reason God keeps sparing my life*, I thought. For what, I didn't know. I simply figured I must have a deeper purpose here on earth, and was thankful to God for another chance to find it.

Not Our Time to Go

In the years my business did well, I was able to purchase season tickets to the Seattle Mariners' games. I was part of a group of four that regularly went, and at various points in time, I had philosophical conversations with each person about the question, "Are we here for a reason?" One person was not convinced there even was a God. Being agnostic, he was open to the possibility that there could be a God, but he was also fine if there is no God.

After the game one night, he and I left with our friends. As we were heading south on Highway 5 in crowded lanes of cars averaging around seventy miles per hour, I was half asleep in the backseat while periodically keeping my eyes open to watch my friend driving. About thirty minutes into the trip, I glanced up to see him jerking the steering wheel to the right, barely avoiding a car that had abruptly swerved into our lane.

The quick jerk of the wheel made the tires squeal. The car darted across the two lanes to the right of us, barely missing cars in those lanes. Now on the far-right shoulder, the car jerked back to the left, cutting across all four lanes. As we neared the center divider, the car then swerved hard right again, and again we were in the far-right shoulder as the car swerved left, and we again swerved before barely missing the retaining wall. As we moved from the far-left lane back toward the shoulder, when we were halfway to the divider yet again, the car suddenly did a 180-degree turnaround. Now traffic was coming directly at us as we sailed backward.

At some point I became aware that I didn't have my seatbelt on, so I grabbed the hand strap while pushing my feet into the passenger seat in front of me. As cars sped toward us, we made a 45-degree turn down an embankment off the shoulder. The car rolled backward down the hillside, coming to a stop between two posts of a chain-link fence, with bushes in front of the fence.

What happened in less than a minute seemed like it took fifteen minutes. Somewhat in shock, I watched my friend release the white-knuckled grip he had on the steering wheel. All I could do was laugh. It a nervous laugh, but it broke the eerie silence that filled the air. Next I blurted out, "Nice job, Curt."

Later I gave him the nickname Speed Racer. It was obvious Curt had no control of the car. He admitted that in swerving to avoid an accident, it was all he could do to hold the wheel to keep the car from flipping over.

After getting out of the car, we all couldn't believe what had just happened. We walked around the car and there wasn't a

HITTING MY STRIDE?

scratch on us or the car. After walking back up the hill, I reached the shoulder of the highway only to see the extent of the miracle that just occurred. How was it that on a busy highway with cars going seventy miles per hour that we were not hit by another vehicle? How was it that in this stretch of highway, there was only one spot that had a clear opening (the spot we went down) and that we didn't hit any barriers, concrete partitions, posts, or guardrails? How did the car go backward after doing a one-eighty and continue to go backward as fast as it had been going forward?

The next day, my friend and I went back to the scene and discovered just how miraculous it was that we had not a scratch on us or the car. Daylight revealed that there was no other opening in the highway for miles, except for the spot we went down. Also, the pitch of the hill surely should have flipped the car. Finally, the car came to rest between two posts of a chain-link fence that only had a few feet on either side of the posts.

I asked my friend what it was like to see cars coming at him, and he said he had been at peace and felt calm. He went on to say it felt like a hand grabbed the back of the car and pulled us backward, guiding us down that hill to our resting place. All I could say was, "It was the hand of God."

Nodding, he agreed, "You know, I think you're right." After further conversations with him, he came to believe in God and that it was not our time to die.

When I learned to reflect on my past, one thing became clear above everything else: My life must matter for something, and I'd better figure it out and do whatever it took to start living it. My soul song had to come alive, and I needed to live from that soul place, not a place of fear. To quote a line from one of my favorite movies, *The Shawshank Redemption,* "I guess it comes down to a simple choice, really. Get busy living or get busy dying."[1]

---

1   "The Shawshank Redemption (1994), *IMDb*, https://www.imdb.com/title/tt0111161/.

Chapter Nine

SURRENDERING TO MY SONG

Figuring that much out didn't make it easy, though. It was a step in the right direction, yet at the same time it didn't tell me which direction to go. You see, I was looking for direction out in the world instead of inside where my soul resided. Since I was not fully aware of this, the best I knew to do was to just keep putting one foot in front of the other and deal with what life put in front of me. Until I connected with my soul and reflected on my journey, which meant truly dealing with the pain of my past, I would never be able to fully live my purpose. That soul connection was what would provide the road map for the future and guide me on my journey in a way that I was not reacting out of pain or my ego, but rather from my soul purpose.

During my journey, many times I felt like God had abandoned me. It wasn't until I went through the dark night of the soul that I would better understand why God lets us experience these times, and it wasn't until I worked for a nonprofit later in my career that I experienced the full impact of my dark night of the soul.

I had achieved monetary success, and from the outside it seemed like I had everything, but there was still a sadness so deep-seated in my soul that it felt unbearable at times. My life was broken by loss, perceived failure, and long-buried emotional wounds that were locked in a lonely, dark place deep within in my being. Feeling the weight of all this was a life-shaking experience that touched my soul itself.

At this point in my career, my Seattle business allowed me to take summers off. I was sitting on the dock of our lake cabin and thought, *Well, God, if you still want to use me in the nonprofit world, here I am, but if you don't need me anymore, I'll be happy to just jet ski and boat all summer.*

Within three days, I received a call from a nonprofit. "Hey, how you been? Haven't talked to you in a while. Can we take you to lunch this week?"

Oh boy, this sounded familiar. I thought, *Here we go again.*

This lunch meeting turned into one of the hardest challenges in my life. I asked, "So how is the nonprofit doing these days?"

"Well, Rich, you see, we're going to close it down this week after helping people for over fifty years. We just can't keep the doors open anymore."

In shock and disbelief, I finally asked, "Well, is there anything I can do to help?"

In my mind I was offering to help close it down, but he responded, "We were hoping you would come in and try to keep it open."

No way, I thought. *No way will I do this*. But deep down in my soul, I knew God wanted me to do it. Frankly, to this day, I don't know why, but I was obedient to what I felt He wanted me to do. Reluctantly, I responded, "Ah, sure, Bob. I can start tomorrow to see what can be done."

Long story short, it cost sixty hours a week of blood, sweat, and tears, but the nonprofit was still open and I felt my job was done. However, during my entire time working there, I felt like I was in a dark night of the soul. While others at the nonprofit couldn't see the invisible memories of my past, they filled me with despair during that season.

It was the decision to be obedient and continue the journey into the dark night of the soul that would eventually lead to growth and a soulful evolution. Despite the hardship of saving an international nonprofit from going out of business, that same process took me from one phase of life into another. It reminded me who is in charge and what it felt like to surrender from the trappings of the world. My mind had been drawn away from my true purpose of serving others and had taken control of my destiny at this point in life. Yet again, I pursued everything that looked like success to the world, abandoning any connection to my spiritual heart and God-given purpose.

Running from my purpose is what led to my needing to go through a dark night of the soul. It was God calling me once again to Himself so I could find the healing I needed and stop going around the mountain again and again. Through this entire season, my mind was saying, "Don't do this!" but my soul was shouting, "Yes! Do this! Your God-given purpose is over here!"

My mind had battled with God and my soul song throughout my life, which explains why half of my career was spent trying to survive while the other half was spent doing nonprofit work. Even though my physical mind and body didn't want to get up every morning at five, trudge up one hundred stairs from my lake house to my car, and drive forty-five minutes to the nonprofit, only to experience extreme spiritual warfare, my soul knew it was part of my divine purpose.

Yes, my lifetime of experience gave me the skills I needed for the job, but I still wasn't fully connecting the dots between my past and my purpose. And, once again, I had to decide whether I would trust God. Just as my whole life had bounced back and forth between running from fear and serving others, it also bounced back and forth between relying on myself and trusting God. At times it was an ongoing battle with no peace of mind or soul to be found.

During my time working to save the nonprofit, I thought about what leadership was and how hard it could be. I bought

SURRENDERING TO MY SONG

a picture of Jesus and hung it on the wall in my office to remind me who I was working for and what leadership looks like. I was inspired by Jesus and what He went through to help mankind.

I also thought of Abraham Lincoln, whose early life was surrounded by death and loneliness, and whose adult life was weighed down by a war in which thousands of young men died. In Lincoln's dark night, he became an icon of wisdom and leadership. He once said, "If there's a worse place than hell, I'm in it."[1]

As I would find out, my experiences of working in tough situations was where my leadership grew. My dark night became a high calling filled with the pain and loneliness of running a nonprofit with no board members in sight; however, this abandonment by the board helped prepare me to recognize my song and my purpose.

The dark night of the soul I'm talking about is an experience in which a person feels totally in the dark about everything in their existence. Everything that they had hoped and worked for seems to be shrouded in darkness. What used to be my identity had been ripped away, even if it was good. There was no path for my soul before me, and very little relief from the confusion and anxiety of being in the dark.

My connection to my soul song had been broken. With the

---

1 "With Malice Toward None: The Abraham Lincoln Bicentennial Exhibition," *Library of Congress*, https://www.loc.gov/exhibits/lincoln/the-presidency.html.

RACE TO THE SKY

loss of connection, the first words out of my mouth were not always the best as I reacted from my independent mind instead of from a soul connected to God. Sometimes the deepest fear in my heart would blurt out, "Why have you forsaken me?" Then I would stare at the picture of Jesus on the wall.

I felt as if there was an uncrossable chasm between myself, God, and my divine purpose on earth, but I would stare at the picture of Jesus anyway to constantly remind myself of who I was working for. I felt emptiness in a way that's hard to describe. Sometimes the pain was so deep that I felt like I would die if I relaxed into it. But this was only a season.

For me, this was a short training. Everything I believed was being questioned, and I felt like I had no earthly support. Yet hope comes in strange, unexplainable forms. If you're asked to bear this experience, know that the rewards will outweigh the grief and sadness you bear. Such persons are in the deepest training to be light bearers in the darkest of places. I did see great miracles as I slowly transcended out of it.

This was my experience, and I would continue to see miracles on my journey if I would stay connected with the Creator on my journey. The only hang-up was I had to trust God so the mission of my soul could come forward again. It was only by the connection of my mind, heart, and soul that I could reconnect to the true purpose for my existence here on earth.

This new consciousness and connectedness was the spark I needed to shine the light that would guide me out of the dark night of the soul.

My Recurring Nightmare

If I was ever going to be able to stick to my guns in trusting God, I had to find a way to overcome my fears. That meant I needed to finally face the trauma of my past—and the fears I'd been running from my entire life. The only question was where to start. What was the source of my fear and why did it persist?

I'm sure you've noticed by now that when I do something, I go all-in. Dealing with my trauma was no different. I tried many different methods—spiritual retreats, counseling, therapy, and more. The truth is, most of the experiences I had stretched me. I had seen God do so many miracles and witnessed so many unexplainable things, but what God did to heal my trauma went even further.

Only a small part of my healing journey is recorded here, just enough to show how God broke through time and time again to help me reconnect to both Him and my own soul. I started with the first memories I had of being afraid—a recurring nightmare from when I was two until I was five.

In this nightmare, I floated down on billowy gray clouds that surrounded me amid pillars of light. The light clouds came together to form an elongated funnel. As I passed through the funnel, I felt as light as a feather; however, the clouds became grayer and closed in on me. Like an army before a battle, the clouds gathered closer together until the darkness engulfed me.

Initially, the dark tunnel was thousands of feet wide and I was still relaxed, but as I continued to float downward, the feeling of comfort transitioned to that ominous feeling one gets before being caught in a terrible storm. The feeling of mild discomfort quickly became a raging storm of fear inside me. The tunnel narrowed and was more confining, bringing a sense of foreboding. More and more fear consumed me. I traveled farther into the tunnel of clouds, and as the clouds became more threatening, my breathing became labored.

Suddenly my descent stopped and I collapsed. The light dimmed and the clouds turned as dark as slate. Black clouds continued to gather, extinguishing the calming light. A loud buzz erupted, followed by a thunderous explosion that brought an outpouring of rain. The water raged in torrents and forced its way down my throat. I was gagging, choking, dying. I felt as though I was drowning. *This must be what death feels like*, I thought.

I choked one last time in my fight to live, then released a ferocious scream and, still screaming, I would sit up in bed in a cold sweat, usually having wet my pants. My nightshirt would be soaked with sweat as I continued screaming at the top of my lungs until my mom would run into my bedroom to comfort me. Only being held by her could help me sleep again, but this nightmare repeated itself for over two years and remained in my subconscious long into my adulthood.

Healing the Trauma

When I determined to address my fears, I attended a spiritual retreat, the goal of which was to help attendees heal from trauma. By the various retreat processes, God led me through what the facilitators called a birth regression experience, in which I uncovered memories leading to and including my birth. What I discovered was that I was reliving my birth through those nightmares.

However, I also learned something deeper somehow—if possible, from even before my birth. The earliest memory I felt God brought up for me seemed to be from a time when my soul understood it was being placed on earth for a purpose, that somehow, even as my body was just beginning to form, my soul understood that I would be born for a reason. I can't explain any of those things, but I can say it was powerful in my life because it concretely established that I really do have a purpose, that there was a reason to not just run from my pain and fears. I resolved to find that purpose and move forward in it.

One of the strangest things about it is I had a sense that my soul knew, even before being born, that the journey would be hard, yet before I met any of those trials, my soul still trusted God. Unfortunately, whatever trust was there was quickly buried. My conscious mind wasn't aware of the trust; it was only aware of experience, and my experiences were painful. Regardless of how quickly that trust was buried, though, knowing it had been there before any of the pain was there gave me a new place to start. Now I had something good that came before any of the bad that had always been my foundation.

After the birth regression experience at the spiritual retreat, the leadership team suggested that I participate in what they called a rebirth experience, basically something through which

God could give me a different, less traumatic start. My birth regression felt healing, so I believed that even though rebirth sounded a bit odd, I probably had nothing to lose. I decided to give it a try, having no idea how difficult it would prove to be.

My experience from the visions I had during my rebirth experience essentially picked up where my nightmare left off, and it felt no less terrifying than when I'd been a child. In fact, I felt just as near death as I had in my nightmares. At times I literally collapsed, paralyzed with fear.

The difference this time was that I could open my eyes and see that I was safe, giving me courage to keep going. As much as everything inside me was crying out, "I don't want to be here! This was a mistake!" I could see a clear-blue light at the end of the tunnel. As crazy as I felt the whole thing was, I kept going, crawling ahead through the process my therapists had suggested.

Finally, I could hear voices encouraging me, saying positive and loving things about my being born. I pressed on toward the light I could see, as an enthusiasm grew around me. I broke through my fears, excited about being born anew. I denounced the vow of not wanting to be here and wondered if my claustrophobia would now also subside.

Sand Tray Therapy

Another moment of clarity came through sand tray therapy, which is a technique that "can be used to facilitate healing in adults, adolescents, and children, allowing them to express their thoughts and feelings when words alone are not enough. In

SURRENDERING TO MY SONG

addition to its therapeutic use, sand tray can be a tool for personal growth and the development of creativity."[2]

I was led to a room filled with small toy figures and other children's toys. In the middle of the room was a large round tray with about a four-foot radius. I was instructed to just take my time and put in the tray anything I wanted from the immense number of figurines and toys. With just those instructions, the facilitator left.

After scanning the thousands of objects around the room, I pulled three off the shelves within thirty seconds, maybe less. One was the Genie figurine from the cartoon movie *Aladdin*, one was Bugs Bunny sitting in a red convertible car, and one was Mickey Mouse sitting in an open carriage with a trailer hitch. The car had a hitch, so, after putting all three objects in the tray, I connected the car to the trailer. With the vast remaining space of sand in the tray, I used my fingers to make wave lines around the figurines, much like waves in the sand going around the center of the figurines. I placed the car, trailer, and Genie in the center of the sand tray.

The facilitator came back and asked, "What does this mean to you?"

I hadn't thought about why I picked only three items or what those objects meant. I considered the question for a minute while looking at the objects, then the answer came to me clearly as I began telling it to the facilitator. "It's simple. The Genie can

---

[2] "I Love Sand Tray Therapy," *Play Therapy with Carmen*, https://www.play-therapywithcarmen.com/collections/i-love-sandtray-therapy/regular-fit.

grant you any wish you ask for, Bugs Bunny can talk his way into or out of any situation, and Micky Mouse is a really good, kind-hearted character that likes to have fun."

"How does it apply to you?" the facilitator responded.

"Well, at the time I picked them, I didn't think about why," I said. "I just quickly felt drawn to them. Now that you ask why, Mickey represents my true self, and Bugs is an identity that helped me survive in life, since he could talk his way out of problems. The last piece, the Genie, has to do with how I believe I can create my own reality and manifest things, much like a wish, so that most anything is possible."

After thinking about my answer, the facilitator said, "That seems very accurate based on your life story. The fact that in such a large tray you only put in three small objects and the rest of it is empty, with just wavy sand all around, could represent that there might have been turmoil going on outside your mother's womb while you were in it. You may have felt lonely as well, which is why you only put three figurines in the tray. The other characters do seem to reflect your personality."

I went into my sand tray session without a plan. I had overheard someone at the retreat talk about it positively, so after lunch I'd asked one of the facilitators about it and she just happened to have time to do it right when I asked. I had no knowledge about it or expectation of what might happen.

Meeting Jesus

During yet another spiritual retreat, I had one of my most significant moments of breakthrough and healing. It came through a therapy technique called eye movement desensitization and reprocessing (EMDR), but the therapist said afterward that my experience wasn't exactly typical for that technique, which makes me believe God simply showed up like He had so many other times in my life.

Like my experience with the sand tray, I had no idea what to expect from this session and just followed my facilitator's instructions. She told me to follow her finger with my eyes from side to side, then to close my eyes and focus inwardly.

In the first movement, I saw in my mind a plastic curtain with a light behind it. I couldn't make out what was behind the light. After a minute or so went by, the facilitator told me to open my eyes and tell her what I experienced. After I explained what happened, she said, "Good. Let's do it again."

In the second movement of EMDR, I was instantly on the other side of the veil with the light. An image of my mom appeared to my left. I felt her love and care for me. That area of my heart felt like something akin to darkness, but it celebrated the bright light. I immediately felt her warmth, her loving presence, even closer, now next to my left cheek. The facilitator told me to open my eyes, and after I explained what happened, she said, "Good. Let's do it again."

In the third movement, I went right back to where I had been, and this is when I realized, by walking toward the light, that the source of the brightest light was Jesus, standing just a few yards in front of me, looking into my eyes with the deepest expression of love and acceptance. I realized that Jesus is someone my soul loves and respects. (You have to remember, despite all I'd seen God do and the times He'd saved me, I still had a lot of baggage from feeling abandoned by Him when He didn't heal my mom, leaving me with my dad, and later, leaving me feeling alone on the streets of New York City.)

As I looked in my vision, my mom stood to the left of Jesus, and next to Him and behind Him were a host of other beings who glowed a fainter hue. They were rows of spirits; I couldn't tell how many. They seemed to be telling me, "You can do it! You can do it!" The feeling was that they were all behind me in my quest to complete my life's mission.

I had no sense of darkness anymore because the area was illuminated by the light of the spirits, but I could still see darkness around me. I felt comfortable there in the darkness, while my consciousness was focused on the center light.

After another minute went by, the facilitator told me, "Open your eyes and tell me what you experienced." After I did, she said, "Good. Let's do it again."

On the fourth movement, all the spirits were gone except for Jesus. He moved slowly yet smoothly backward; there was no walking involved, just an effortless motion. As He did this, His light created a path of light with darkness all around. The path meandered side to side and then faded out of sight.

The best way I can describe this place is that I felt totally known but totally accepted and loved, and that it made me feel safe and happy. I perceived this place as timeless and spaceless. Distance was expansive, beyond what my normal sight could perceive. Jesus spoke to me thought to thought: "You must go

SURRENDERING TO MY SONG

back. It is not time for you to come here. You have more to do." I wanted to stay because I felt so full of joy and so peaceful, but Jesus repeated, "It is not your time. You have a purpose to fulfill." Though I couldn't see them anymore, all the other spirits were cheering me on, "You can do it! You can do it!"

I would later receive confirmation of what I needed to do, but even then an impression came through to me. From the vision it was clear that my path was to follow Jesus and my journey was not yet over. The only way to follow the path I had seen in my vision was to trust God to lead me down it.

It might seem insignificant to others, but there is one other detail from my vision that's of huge importance to me: I was surrounded by people who were all encouraging me that I can do it. Yes, my mother's death was radically traumatizing, but what really drove home that trauma and compounded it year after year was being alone, having no one to care for or help me. It was being alone that convinced me I could rely only on myself, that made me feel I needed to run in fear and outwork everyone else to avoid ending up like one of the homeless people in New York City.

This vision helped me see that I wasn't alone—and that I'd never been alone. It showed me that, in some sense, my mom had always been with me, cheering me on, right along with Jesus. Most importantly, this and other supernatural experiences I have shared of my journey showed me that God was not only with me but that He also loved me just the way I am and can meet me—and all of us—right where I am since He is a God of love.

RACE TO THE SKY

What About Bob?

I had been going hard after finding healing from my trauma for a few years when an opportunity came up and put to the test just how healed I really was. After not seeing family members, including my father, for three decades, an invitation that shook me to my core came in the mail; it was to my Aunt Dot's ninetieth birthday party in Florida. My apprehension was not so much due to seeing my aunts and cousins, but because my estranged dad would be there, and he was dying.

Thirty years is a long time to not see someone. Having not seen him or talked to him for that long implied that there were taboo subjects that would be difficult to discuss. His sitting there dying was one of those subjects, not to mention the things he did to or didn't do for me as a kid.

Flying the many hours to Florida gave me a lot of time to think. *Will I actually see my dad at this event after all these years? Will he be dead before I get there? If he is there, will I even talk with him?*

When I arrived with a bouquet of flowers, my aunt thought I was the flower delivery boy. It had been nearly forty years since I'd last seen her. After explaining who I was, she greeted me with a warm hug. After my mom's death, I had been dropped off at many relatives' homes. I had warm memories—of what a strong matriarch can be in a household and how she would play endless games with us. Her home was where I learned how to play poker, with all the New York slang that goes with the game. It was nice to see her and my cousins once again.

SURRENDERING TO MY SONG

Her son got up during the event and spoke about all the amazing things she did for her family. It moved me to see the blessing a mother can be to her children and family when she can simply be present and active in their lives. I knew I had been deprived of that blessing, but I was touched that much more because of my loss.

In a room the size of a banquet hall, with about eighty people scattered about, I saw the profile of a man I once knew. Sitting across the room from him, I was looking at a gaunt shadow of the man I used to call Dad. The chair next to him was empty, and as I walked closer to his table, I saw he had become a frail old man. Seeing him with my own eyes only solidified the fact that he was dying. The idea of losing both my parents to cancer, even fifty years apart, was a harsh reality of life. To be honest, I struggled to cope with it.

I sat down in the empty chair next to him. He turned toward me with drooping gray eyes that used to be blue. I could only see a sad person who never really should have had kids. Stating the name he knew me by a kid, I said, "I'm Rick, your son."

Being half deaf, he kept saying, "Who are you?"

I would repeat who I was, only for him to say, "Who is this?" to the rest of my aunts sitting around the table.

He finally said to my Aunt Dot, "Who the heck is this, Dot?"

"It's your son, Rick!" she blurted out. "Phil, it's your son!"

What he said to me next came out in an alarmed, surprised voice: "No, really, who are you?"

Giving up, I said, "I'm Bob."

Now he was really confused. Why I said Bob, I'm not sure,

but it was odd to have my own dad not know who I was for a solid seven minutes. Sitting there talking as Bob for a while, I brought up things only he and I would know until I believe he finally recognized me.

"Your eyes. Yes, your eyes," he said. "You have your mother's eyes. You are my son."

From there, I listened to about ten minutes of insults, lies, and insinuations that he had made up about me and had come to truly believe about the past. This is a typical behavior with lying alcoholics. He was denying the truth that now unexpectedly sat in front of him as he was near death. He had to deny the truth and stand up for the false reality of stories that he now convinced himself were truth. The reason he lied so much is because he was an alcoholic and was filled with shame. He knew deep down inside that he abandoned his children and had not been there for me.

One of the most frustrating things for me was how he could deny factual events and only remember whatever truths were convenient to him. He would make up stories to fill in the blanks between reality and the trauma I experienced. Frankly, before his death he didn't even know many of the things I went through, since I never had a relationship with him. He refused to admit the truth or reality of the conditions I was subjected to. In his mind, he was Saint Phil, a victim of being stuck with two kids after his wife's death.

When I talked about being in trauma for many years and how I had adapted my whole life in response to his alcoholism, he replied, "I was never an alcoholic. I only went to Alcoholics

SURRENDERING TO MY SONG

Anonymous for my crazy second wife's sake. She's the one who was an alcoholic and addicted to pills. It was never me that had a problem."

As I sat there and listened to his fictional reality of the past, I felt only pity for him. I finally just said, "I'm sorry if I hurt you in any way."

Yes, forgiveness. I reached forgiveness! Man, was it freeing! After enduring another verbal assault, I again said that I was sorry if I hurt him in any way. A sudden shift came over him. He changed from attack mode to wanting to know about me and my life.

I wanted to do the right thing, to win back some dignity that the relationship had never had before. He was dying, and this would be the last time I would see him. So we talked about many things, from sports to the weather. Since silence didn't serve the interests of either of us, I continued to talk about almost anything except the spiritual journey I had been on for so many years.

Memories of my early life started flashing in my mind—of a man who looked different thirty, forty, and fifty-plus years ago. I wondered, *Should I tell him that I've considered suicide, become religious, feared failure, or changed my priorities in life? Should I ask him if he fears dying, if he has any regrets, or whether he believes in an afterlife? Is he happy or depressed about dying? Does he wish he had taken more risks? Does he wish he'd spent more time with his family? Given that he is dying, what will he miss the most? How does he want to be remembered?* Instead, I kept it light and talked about the New York Yankees. He shared that he met Babe Ruth once as a kid in the city. The Babe said to him, "Hey kid, how are you?" as he brushed by my dad on the street, stepping out of a cab he had just pulled up in.

Then I wondered if my dad had ever had a bucket list and if he achieved what was on it. Did he know his song and did he get to sing it? The reality of how short life is and how we need to seize the moment became more real than ever. What's sad is that many of us never know our song in this lifetime.

Since the age of five, when I learned my mom had cancer, my one true ambition in life was to survive through a life full of trauma. As I heal from it all, I find it is therapeutic to reflect on my life through this amazing creative outlet called writing.

Writing has helped me see things for what they were, and still makes it bearable to move past those traumas. As a schoolboy I ran for fun, then for survival. Now I run through the act of writing, allowing even a few lines to heal my universe. As I reflect, I realize I'm writing a screenplay of my life. At times it's cathartic and other times it's painful, but it seems to promote the healing process by looking at the truth and not running away from it.

It seems surreal, like a movie. In trying to organize multiple traumas that led to living in a constant state of fear, I could see the journey made me into a survivor, someone who must forgive and let his shield down. I realized that now I must love someone who abandoned me in my most crucial time in life.

When I started talking about good memories with my dad, the few I could remember, it brought him great joy. In that moment I realized this was about releasing many things that I couldn't see but could feel—letting go of anger, bitterness, and resentment. I knew this would change my life and clear the road for my future path to live free of the bondage of unforgiveness that helped keep my soul in prison.

That is what I'm doing now—making a shape for the rest of my life before death, so that I (and others) can see it clearly. We must forgive those who have hurt us the most, to be free ourselves. This is what I want to do in the last chapters of my life, to forgive and live life to the fullest, to live up to my soul's song and who God created me to be.

As my dad smiled with deeply yellow-stained teeth from the chemo and old age, he invited me to lunch the next day at Bob Evans.

There it was again. The night before I was Bob, and now I was eating at Bob's with my dad. He made jokes that made no sense, as he was losing his mind, but I laughed anyway, and as we said our goodbyes outside, tears of sadness welled up and poured out of me. Weeping and sobbing flowed like a broken dam of thirty years of pent-up tears.

My dad said many kind things—how much he thought about me over the years and how proud he was of me and how he couldn't cry because of the chemo. He couldn't taste or feel anything or even cry, but his words were sincere. As we said our final goodbye, I helped him to his car. He drove away, crashing into the curb but smiling. I'd offered to drive, but maybe it was his pride or dignity that wouldn't allow me to drive him the one block to the assisted living center where he was staying.

It made me think, *How will I go out?* I hope to go out well, and peacefully, maybe even surrounded by friends and family, to finish my journey strong with my head up high. Yet, as I write this, my soul is still scared to come out of hiding. My old identities hang on with the fear.

"I can't die," they cry out. "Not me. Not now." But they must die if I am to become what God made me to be.

Yes, I have regrets, but as soon as I start writing about my past, I realize how my perceived failures and mistakes are not what define me. Take regrets away and you're nothing since you need them to learn and grow. But I do wonder where I'd be now if I'd made different choices—if I'd been bolder, smarter, surer of what I wanted and how to get it.

As it was, running in fear, making life up as I went along, was an incredible experience since I was flying by the seat of my pants. Now, though, I see clearly that I can trust God. He loves me, and He has great plans for my life. We all give great pleasure to God since He created us in His image. Galatians 1:15 says, "But even before I was born, God chose me and called me by his marvelous grace. Then it pleased him" (NLT).

My identity was wrapped around being married, having children, and then trying to change the reality I had lived up to that point. To become a father is to die to oneself in some essential way. After I had children, I assumed the role of *Father Knows Best*. I became a hero dad, having to move on and take on his true identity.

No, I'm not likely to take more risks in life now that I am getting older, but calculated adventure sure sounds good. I may tackle skydiving or paragliding, but not bull riding. The biggest calculated risk is letting go of what I know and embracing my soul song—and letting go of fear, learning to trust God again, and embracing the future journey He has for me.

Generational Blessings and Curses

The entire unfolding of what happened in my family is incredible to me. My father never really knew his father, each of them thrown into a city during difficult times. My grandfather was forced to work some of the most dangerous jobs imaginable yet he survived. Despite his surviving, however, he never became a true father and didn't raise my dad.

My dad repeated the same mistakes while being thrown into New York during some of the darkest days in her history. He was a cop and at the forefront of the gang wars and drug sales, the serial killers and the layoffs. As a result of his upbringing and what he faced, he rejected fatherhood as well, leaving me to figure out the city by myself.

Praise God for television, because those early shows I watched planted a seed inside me to know what fatherhood ought to be. If it weren't for those examples, and for God's direct intervention in key moments, I'm sure I would have done the same thing my grandfather and father had done before me.

This pattern was clearly a generational curse working its way through my family line, growing with each generation until it got to me and I couldn't take it anymore. By God's grace and mercy, that curse is broken in my family.

In its place is a generational blessing, which my grandfather unknowingly also began. I never knew it for years, until my sister told me about our grandpa building Rockefeller Center in 1932. He had been with me and inspiring me for years, and he literally paved the way I took in leaving New York.

On my moms' side, the little I knew of my other grandfather was that he was a professional athlete and was also in the Olympics. His name was Rudolf Korner. He was also an incredibly warm-hearted person who was very generous and caring, from him I inherited all of those generational blessings, which served me well in sports and in life. Even though my father blocked this relationship by wrongly throwing him out of our house while he was in a drunken rage after my mom died, my mom's father served as one of the only role models I had, even if it was from a distance since I knew little else about him.

The Bible speaks of God as our Father, and if our earthly examples are bad ones, it skews and taints the way we see God. In my case, my dad abandoned me, so I expected God to do the same. But if our father is a good example, it will usher us into strong connection to God as our Father. This is the ultimate benefit of having generational blessings at work in your family and getting rid of generational sins. The sins will always lead us to be bad examples and put up roadblocks to our truly knowing God as our Father, but the blessings coming from healthy fathers will keep driving us to know God better, believing He is truly and genuinely good.

This is finally where I am. I can both see and own my past without holding on to the pain, trauma, fear, and bitterness it gave me. I have clear vision and my sights set on fulfilling my

SURRENDERING TO MY SONG

soul song, living the purpose for which I was born. The road I've walked has been difficult, but I am now equipped like few others to help those who have also walked painful roads.

That is my purpose—to help others find their soul song and live it fully, free from any pain that would hold them back—and with God's continued help, I will see it to the end.

Chapter Ten

LEARNING HOW TO LOVE

In looking at my life's journey thus far, I have learned that God is not a God of fear but rather a God of love who has guided me. Despite living most of my life from a place of fear and unforgiveness, God still showed up to save me from myself and near-death situations. I had to learn to trust Him again in order to be free from fear.

In New York City culture, if someone wrongs you, they're put in the non-trust category. In other words, "You're dead to me." What about the idea of forgiveness? "Forget about it."

This mindset became part of my DNA. The old saying that you can take the kid out of New York, but you can't take New

York out of the kid seemed to apply to my survival mentality. Constantly running from the fear of winding up like the homeless created a drive that would never let me rest. This kept me running on the hamster wheel of life, which led to nowhere.

Isolating Yourself from God and the World

One of my theme songs of my youth was Simon and Garfunkel's "I Am a Rock." The message that a rock feels no pain and an island never cries was one I could relate to. I had cut off all my feelings and emotions, refusing access to my heart and soul. Becoming a rock was a protective identity I adopted because I no longer felt safe being "me."

After leaving the nonprofit world and having gained some measure of success, I was still isolating myself from people, from society, and from the purpose for which I was born. People hurt me, not only in the nonprofit world but also in other areas of business and in my personal life. By choosing not to forgive and hiding my soul away, my unique gifts were not being used to contribute back to society. When I realized that we are all flawed, critical, and judgmental, I was able to forgive myself and others in order to engage back into life and my soul purpose. That is where my fulfillment resided, in being able to live—and live from my own soul song.

Isolating myself from others and God kept me away from my soul blueprint and serving with my gifts in society. We all have unique gifts that have been put into our soul blueprint. By learning to be who we were designed to be, we become a natural asset to this planet and beyond. God's design is for these gifts to be given to others and for all of us to use all of our unique gifts for the good of society.

We all go through pain and trauma in our life, but if we stay connected and don't withdraw from God, we can begin to heal. God is love and acceptance, and His design is for all of us to use our gifts and live a rich, rewarding life. By staying connected to our heart, soul, and God, we can live a life that has fulfillment and acceptance. God accepts us right where we are on our journey.

Personally, knowing and following God's still small voice had made living my life worth it, especially as I have learned to hear His voice and follow it. Having faith that God has the best plan for our lives brings great peace and comfort. This revelation of how unique and gifted we all are, and the awareness to walk with Him in trust moment by moment, is what frees us from all the fears that hold us back from living out our true purpose.

Look at all the beauty God has created in this world. It's not just the wonders of the world, the animals, the flowers, the peacocks, the sunsets, the butterflies, the rainbows, and the goodness found in each of us, but it is also the synchronicity found in nature that truly shows the nature of God and that there is a design for things in this world that God has put in place. He has paid for and given us free will to choose this relationship with Him, to walk in the soul's alignment, the unique personalized blueprint He has placed in each and every one of us.

RACE TO THE SKY

Protective Identities

My false bravado of creating protective identities happened because I felt unsafe to be my natural, free self. Gabrielle Roth, an American dancer and musician in the world-music and trance-dance genres, with a special interest in shamanism, explained this loss of identity in an explanation where she stated, "In many shamanic societies, if you came to a medicine person complaining of being disheartened, dispirited, or depressed, they would ask one of four questions: 'When did you stop dancing? When did you stop singing? When did you stop being enchanted by stories? When did you stop being comforted by the sweet territory of silence?'"[1]

When I experienced loss, I shifted my identity and core self-esteem to protect myself from the fear of becoming destitute and abandoned. I desperately obsessed about achievement, accomplishments, and being a successful businessperson, consultant, and entrepreneur, which led me to invest my energy in accomplishing goals at the expense of enriched relationships and activities that fed my soul. I was succeeding out of fear.

Consequently, my world was practically turned upside down every time goals were not achieved since I perceived these as failure, and failure was not an option for me. Being very goal oriented, I could manifest things, but what I was missing was the complete manifestation of God's fulfilling adventure for my life.

---

1 "Gabrielle Roth > Quotes > Quotable Quotes," *Goodreads*, https://www.goodreads.com/quotes/2070054-in-many-shamanic-societies-if-you-came-to-a-medicine.

LEARNING HOW TO LOVE

What held me back was fear of trusting that God's plan might be better than my plan of achieving man-made things that had no deep long-lasting meaning.

Fear and survival forces us into protective identities and careers that are often not in alignment with our soul blueprint and true calling in life. Each person has a divine, instinctive awareness of how special and crucial their authentic identity is. Instead of outright rejecting our organic identity, we hide it away deep in our subconscious—so deep that we find it almost impossible to realign with it without wise assistance. Living in fear and not being connected with our soul identity and soul purpose pushes us in the direction of reactivity and conformity, not purpose. Not living from our authentic identity is tiring and creates unnecessary anxiety and dissatisfaction, plus it shortens life.

A deep connection with the Designer of our authentic self will reconnect us with our organic self. We awaken and discover our life vision and purpose. It becomes easier to follow the cry of our soul as we learn to listen deeply.

We need to push past fear and be willing to dive into the field of unknown possibilities. In this field we can manifest things that go beyond our own ability, since we are one with the source of life, the Creator. This enlightened path may seem crazy and risky, and there may be tremendous fear of unknown possibilities; after all, it may not follow the roads commonly traveled by others and fit society's rules for success and expectations. But if we push past the fears, we become one with God and His purpose for our life, submerging our soul in a sea of tranquility.

RACE TO THE SKY

The Spirit speaks through our soul and provides us wisdom, compassion, and a guiding light that is our inner teacher (as promised by the Master Teacher). If we tune in and listen, we can connect and find our sense of meaning and purpose.

When we live "in connection" with Creator, in harmony with the design He originated, even our emotions and awareness have a different tuning and purpose. Darkness, anxiety, and fear provide us with valuable information, both inwardly and outwardly; they are now tools for growth and service. Part of this fulfillment comes when we wake up every day knowing we're not going to work just for sustenance, but instead because our career is illuminating a pathway for our soul to shine, since it is expressing itself for all who seek the true calling of their lives. That is being in alignment with our soul blueprint.

Through awakening experiences and wise individuals who helped guide my journey home, I realized I would never be alone again. God will always be with me. This realization of always having God with me changed my life dramatically since I could be at peace knowing He was in me and with me always. I could let go of the fear of man and man-made things, and stop hanging on to worldly things so desperately. It made me aware of the fact that our time here in this world is brief, but our soul and the things of the heart, along with our connection to God, are timeless.

It is in this connection with God that we find our purpose and fulfillment. Having a purpose and a reason to get out of bed even increases our life span. According to WebMD, people who retire at fifty-five are 89 percent more likely to die in the ten years after retirement than those who retire at sixty-five. I believe the reason is they have lost their vision and purpose of being here.

If we're not in connection with God and our soul, we're not being fed positive thoughts and messages that fill our being. Instead we're subjected to fear and the many negative thoughts that fill our mind. According to *Psychology Today*, "between 60 and 70 percent of the average students' spontaneously occurring thoughts are negative. ... Each of these categories of mental chatter is, I believe, rooted in goals and values to which most of us blindly subscribe. As such, it's not surprising that our thoughts revolve around inferiority, love, and control. For example, most of us are brought up to succeed and excel in life."[2]

According to the Mayo Clinic, "we can stop negative self-talk to reduce stress. Positive thinking helps with stress management and can even improve your health. Practice overcoming negative self-talk. Is your glass half-empty or half-full? How you answer this age-old question about positive thinking may reflect your outlook on life, your attitude toward yourself, and whether you're optimistic or pessimistic—and it may even affect your health."[3]

Imagine if we could flip-flop the number of positive thoughts to be 70 percent positive instead of negative. Connecting with

---

2 Raj Ragunathan, PhD, "How Negative Is Your 'Mental Chatter'?" *Psychology Today*, October 10, 2013, https://www.psychologytoday.com/us/blog/sapient-nature/201310/how-negative-is-your-mental-chatter.

3 Mayo Clinic Staff, "Positive thinking: Stop negative self-talk to reduce stress," February 18, 2017, https://www.mayoclinic.org/healthy-lifestyle/stress-management/in-depth/positive-thinking/art-20043950.

RACE TO THE SKY

God can give you these results. According to Bruce Davis, Ph.D., "each day the average person has about 50,000 thoughts. Some researchers put that number at 70,000 thoughts per day. On the other side of the wall is everything but stillness. There is the backlog of complaints, concerns, worries, difficult feelings, lots and lots of thought, everything but peace and quiet. Healing begins in any activity that is without the expectation of talking, with no demands to finish the unfinished conversation. When there are no expectations, we can enjoy the peace and quiet. The heart is free to soften and open. A quiet mind makes for an available heart."[4]

Being able to slow down and connect with the heart and then the soul, we can begin a dialogue with God. That journey of two-way communication with the Creator not only changes our thoughts but also changes our action. During this communication with our soul awareness, we become clear about our purpose. This alignment with our soul purpose can then create new dialogue for the mind, giving us positive thoughts that help us create clear vision and actions for our lives.

During my healing process, God showed me a vision of what happened spiritually when I received the news, at the age of nine, that my mom's second mastectomy didn't stop the spread of her cancer. He showed me that the harsh reality of this news opened the door for the spirit of death to reside in our house.

---

4 Bruce Davis, Ph.D., "There Are 50,000 Thoughts Standing Between You And Your Partner Every Day!" May 23, 2013, https://www.huffpost.com/entry/healthy-relationships_b_3307916.

This uninvited guest created a new fear and loneliness that I had never felt before, which not only forced my soul into hiding, but also severed my faith and connection with God. My soul's hiding place became a prison.

Who knew then that it would be a life sentence, filled with many paroled excursions when my soul would be released for good behavior? Going in and out of soul prison was challenging, since there were no programs to rehabilitate my soul into a healed state so it could be released for good. From my mid-twenties on, my ability to stay connected to my soul and have clear communication from God was difficult at best. Fear, uncertainty, and not being able to trust God were the reasons my mind overrode my soul's cry.

Now in my fifties, I stand at crossroads. Do I dare to let my soul come out of hiding for good and finally decide to take God seriously, or do I keep going in and out of soul prison for the rest of my life, never having fulfilled my true purpose and all of God's plan for my life?

The soul blueprint that God put in me when my life began is part of my journey. It's time to stay connected to the Creator's call and not let the distractions of life derail my destiny. Having spent many years trying to make money, it's time for me to let the old habit structures die and start a new journey of trusting God like never before. Society leads us to believe that man-made constructs and money are the answer and will save us, but the truth is that only when we learn to fully trust God will we be free to walk with Him in His plan for us.

Connecting with God

This is ultimately where God's vision led me. He showed me that my soul went into hiding because it didn't feel safe, but that if I wanted, He would reach into that deep, dark, subterranean cavern far underground where my soul was still hiding, and He would be safe. I needed to trust God again, to let my soul out of hiding. Seeing this truth from God's perspective, I reached out to Him and prayed that He would protect my soul. It's not like I was ever really protected anyway, having forgotten it was even there.

As God shapes us on our journey, we have free will and make choices that may not always be the best decision. If we can learn from these experiences, they help shape us as we learn, grow, and evolve for the limited time we are here on earth.

Accepting God's free gift of being His friend and having deep relationship with Him is transformative in itself. This transformation leads to our letting go of familiar yet unbeneficial habits and replacing them with new habits in alignment with our Creator-designed soul identity that will help us be our best self. This new soul identity will bring rich joy and fulfillment in life. Our unique design and nature become an asset and opens the door for contribution to the rest of the world.

It is in our connection with God that we discover our soul blueprint. He is the one who helps us see our dreams and visions, and walks with us in them to manifest our divine purpose, if we decide to take the journey with Him. The world lies to us about what matters most, and if we buy these lies, we'll

LEARNING HOW TO LOVE

start an endless journey of trying to find enough yet always feeling like we need more. The never-ending striving to have more doesn't give us peace; instead, we become more imprisoned until we realize that trusting ourselves will never give us what we really need. Only trusting God, connecting with His love for us, will do this.

If we can reconnect to God and our soul's purpose, we can then deal with situations that may cause fear in a nonreactive state. The peace and understanding that comes from knowing God intimately leads to the awareness that God is a God of love and blessing. In this love there's no fear, only a peace that we're protected by an amazing God who is all-knowing and all-loving. There is no greater feeling or experience than walking with our Creator who knows us and only wants the best for us.

If you haven't started this journey yet, it is simple to begin. All you have to do is make the decision that you want a relationship with God. He loves each and every one of us, and is longing to have intimate connection with you.

Walking, talking, and living with God is our ultimate fulfillment while we're here. It's what we all seek, but sometimes in the wrong places. The key is to grow into divine love and trust, where the Lover and the beloved become one. The Creator and the creation become one. This is the place where peace, rest, and gratitude reside; there is no room for fear. When the finite and the Infinite become one, all things become possible through Him and in Him.

Being raised Catholic, I thought I had to go through a priest to have a relationship with God. Instead, I've learned that not only can I have a direct relationship with God, but that it is what He wants for all of us. When we become enlightened to this truth, our path toward our soul blueprint is illuminated. We fully understand that God isn't just a concept written in a book. He is not the dogma of religion. He is not a God waiting to punish us because we aren't good enough. He is not a distant being waiting for us to die so he can punish or reward us.

Rather, He becomes a God who is no longer just a hope. He becomes an actual friend and constant companion you can laugh and cry with. This connection will change your life right now. You don't have to wait days, months, or years. It is an obtainable achievable goal right now. Through talking and listening to God, you jump into the sea of spiritual tranquility where you're one with God and all of creation. Love yourself. Love God with all your heart and soul. Have faith in Him.

This will be my new quest. My true wealth in Him is the ultimate reality and resides not in fear but in the heart of knowing this simple truth. It is where I can be free from the prison my soul may be hidden away in. This journey is to reconnect with God in divine love—to not only pray for what I need but to meet with God as a friend who created my soul, to have relationship with Him and listen for His plan. He wants to be my friend and He loves me. He knows what is best for my life's journey; I just have to listen. And if I listen to Him through my heart and soul connection, I can find the answers I need to be in alignment with Him.

It is in the depth of my soul that I find peace, silence, and a connection with God. All fear, insecurities, doubt, distractions, and inner turmoil melts away amid the peace of being connected by His love to Him and, in some way, to everyone.

Climb Every Mountain

While on a retreat, one of the ministers felt God leading him to share a song with me. He didn't know what the song had meant to me as a child, but said, "I don't know why I keep getting this song for you, but I do. It's 'Climb Every Mountain' from the movie *The Sound of Music*."

I wept and wept. What he didn't know was that this was a song my mom would often sing, from one of her favorite movies.

The song reminded me that I was destined to climb this mountain. There were many paths and choices to get to the top of the mountain, but my destiny and soul song was to reach the top. As my journey has caused the mountain to grow and shift, evolving as I evolved, my challenge has been to be true to my soul purpose, which is who God created me to be. As I continue on this journey, my soul and spirit are excited to see what paths the journey will take me on up to the top of this mountain.

If I stay connected to who God created me to be, that will be my legacy; it will be my voice. It lives in me, so when times are bad, I must make a choice to not forget who I am. God lives in me as well, and if I choose to trust Him, then I can be free of the distractions and lies that cloud my mind and spirit. Trusting God is the way to be set free from the confines of fear.

That has been my journey, to learn how to forgive God and live life from a place of trusting in Him—and to not only trust

Him, but to also have a fun and adventurous relationship with Him outside of the constructs of rigid religion. If I can forgive, love, and trust God again, then my life will finally be fulfilled. There will no longer be that void or need to accomplish more. I can simply rest in knowing that He is my friend whom I can trust, and have fun with and to finally come to peace with Him and myself. The Creator of all things who created me is certainly able to meet my needs every day. I just need to trust Him again so I can have peace at last.

Writing this book forced me to look at what really happened to me instead of pretending I never went through eleven of the profound thirteen traumas of life by the age of thirteen. This truth forced me to look at the fact that I had cut off my emotions and not lived from my connection to God. Finding the courage to heal from the wounds, love myself, love God again, and surrender my will and trust to Him is the challenge I (and all of us) face.

Despite the pain and suffering brought about by other humans, we can have the wisdom of Jesus and unconditionally love others despite their limitations. We are all connected and all created by the same Creator, regardless of religion, nationality, or skin color. Do we see all individuals as hurting people on their own journey? Do we see them as wounded people who need to learn to forgive and love? Can we be observers of why people act the way they do and try to help them by not reacting to their pain (which, in many cases, is directed at us)? That is my challenge today.

Despite all the struggles and people who can make daily life difficult, can we learn from each experience and still forgive and love? Even though humans will hurt us and create distrust, can we still go beyond the pain and see others as God sees us? Can we model love and forgiveness?

Climb Your Mountain

For me, climbing my mountain looks like getting up again when I get knocked down, and not giving up on my journey with God that has led me to knowing my purpose. Climbing my mountain means not letting the naysayers stop me from making the right choices as I strive to fulfill my life's purpose. It looks like choosing to validate people and build them up instead of tearing them down, choosing to handle situations with forgiveness and love instead of merely reacting from emotions. It means I keep in mind that what I give to others will ripple farther out into the world, multiplying whatever contribution I make.

Because of all this, I believe that climbing my mountain looks simply like helping others climb theirs. That's why I wrote this book, and it's why I also help organize and conduct retreats and seminars where people can begin their journey, discover their vision, and clarify what next steps to take. If, having read my story, you realize that you're not living your life's purpose or that you've lost the intimate connection to God you were made to enjoy, we have resources that can help you.

Most humans have abandoned part or all of their original Creator-designed nature. The result is formulating a personality that protects while hiding your original nature deep in your soul's consciousness. The knowledge of these principles and applying what you learn here can and probably will bring difficult decisions and life changes to you and those you love. You may have to leave behind perceived comforts, but in order to evolve and grow on the spiritual journey, change is required.

If you want to live a fulfilled life, you have to make the decision to change and grow. That means deciding to take the journey of a lifetime. It will require letting go of self-formed protective personalities. Being in alignment with your soul purpose will be the most profound journey of your life. Like anything that helps you evolve and grow, there will be times of discomfort as you get set in your ways, making change along your path uncomfortable at times.

The phantom of fear that grips many of us will have to be faced. You can choose to run from your destiny your entire life, or you can make that life-changing decision to face the things you have been avoiding. Your perception that change will bring only pain and discomfort can be replaced with the reality of knowing when you're in alignment with your soul purpose, it will bring fulfillment that comes with great joy.

Believe in Your Vision and the Rest Is Time and Effort

When you find your true soul identity and believe in it, the rest is time and effort. Finding your true self and believing in your vision will manifest when you're in alignment with your soul blueprint. You'll find joy and happiness in walking in your soul blueprint, and it'll also develop a sense of not being alone, and a realization that you're a worthy, talented, capable person who deserves to be loved. And the most important person to believe that is you. Since you're connected with your soul and thus the Creator, you'll never be alone again. God is always with us in the good and bad times; He is our refuge in the storms of life.

What's Next

It took a lifetime of trials for me to get to the point of being in alignment with my soul blueprint, but as I've grown and evolved further in my purpose, I have been developing seminars with Randy Russel of Inner Path Works to help people go through their own soul evolution. We call these seminars Discovering Your Song.

The three seminars are powerful experiences that can help you walk in alignment with God and His purpose for you in life.

1. Seminar One: Discovering Your Soul Self
2. Seminar Two: Living Your Soul Self
3. Seminar Three: Designing the Life Plan to Support Your Soul Blueprint and True Identity

Learning and practicing what is taught at these seminars will lead to fulfilling your destiny. To learn more about where and when our next seminars will be, go to DiscoveringYourSong.com.

God created each of us for a purpose. It took me fifty years of running from trauma, fear, and pain to find mine, but because of that experience, I can tell you how wonderful it is to stop running and surrender to the peace of trusting God to help me live my purpose.

You have your own story, with your own unique contribution to give the world. He will help you realize your dreams and visions for your life. He will help you climb your mountain.

The only question is, will you trust Him?

Do it today. He will lead you to your soul purpose and the fullness of life.

ACKNOWLEDGEMENTS

In our defining moments, God sometimes brings help to guide and shape our journey. I would like to thank my mom, whose influence has been so profound that it has continued even after her passing; John Sandford, a spiritual leader who pioneered the inner-healing movement globally and has now passed on; and Randy Russell, who helped shape this book and is truly a divinely inspired human who continues to help many find their soul song in life. In working with Randy and John, I was and am able to witness true servants of God who live their life according to God's plan for them.

ABOUT THE AUTHOR

Rich Joy owned multiple businesses and worked as a Fortune 500 consultant and a 501(c)(3) consultant before starting his own international company. As his name indicates, he likes to have a lot of fun in life through joking and fulfilling his soul blueprint, which is where he gets his true joy.

To learn more about Rich's next book, workbooks, and additional resources, please visit his website at DiscoveringYourSong.com. You can also register for seminars and sign up for quarterly newsletters.